Proficiency Check
Study Guide

Ace the IPC

James D. Price
ATP, CFII / MEI
Retired Airline Captain
Colonel, USAFR (Retired)

http://www.JDPriceCFI.com

2. GPS domestic en route and terminal IFR operations can be conducted as soon as proper avionics systems are installed, provided all general requirements are met. The avionics necessary to receive all of the ground-based facilities appropriate for the route to the destination airport and any required alternate airport must be installed and operational. Ground-based facilities necessary for these routes must also be operational.

(a) GPS en route IFR RNAV operations may be conducted in Alaska outside the operational service volume of ground-based navigation aids when a TSO-C145a or TSO-C146a GPS/WAAS system is installed and operating. Ground-based navigation equipment is not required to be installed and operating for en route IFR RNAV operations when using GPS WAAS navigation systems. All operators should ensure that an alternate means of navigation is available in the unlikely event the GPS WAAS navigation system becomes inoperative.

This guide is intended to help pilots gather the necessary information needed to help prepare for possible questions that could be asked by examiners and instructors in an Instrument Proficiency Check.

This publication is printed for informational purposes only, and is not intended to substitute for any approved aircraft flight manual, Flight Service briefing, competent flight instruction, or an official government publication. The navigational charts used herein are not current and should not be used for navigation.

Limitation of Liability

ISBN 978-1-938586-82-8

Printed in the United States of America
Writers Cramp Publishing
http://www.writerscramp.us

Other books by James D Price

Flight Review Study Guide will be the first thing you open when getting ready for any pilot proficiency training. Wings flights, or BFR – everything is covered. **The Flight Review Study Guide** is also an indispensable cross county flight-planning handbook. You'll fly with confidence and you'll be a better pilot.

ISBN 978-1-938586-81-1

Aircraft Expense Tracking - Single or Multi, Sole Owner or Club. Aircraft Expense Tracking will help you keep perfect records. You can record aircraft squawks, and keep track of maintenance and oil changes. There's even a spot to record VOR checks and GPS data updates each month.

With **Aircraft Expense Tracking,** you'll always know when inspections are due, how much your aircraft costs per year, and you'll be ready for taxes with business and charitable deductions.

ISBN 978-1-938586-80-4

For more information or to chat with Jim, visit his website at:

http://www.JDPriceCFI.com

Printed in the U.S.A.
http://www.WritersCramp.us

Acknowledgements:

Mooney Aircraft photos, courtesy of Mooney Aircraft Company, Kerrville, TX

Garmin images, courtesy of Garmin, Inc., Olathe, KS

I am grateful to my dear wife Gerry, who encouraged me and helped me find the right words.

Thanks to my friend Phil Corman, who liberally donated massive amounts of enthusiasm, and thoughtful, constructive, criticism.

I express my eternal gratitude to every pilot that I have flown with, whether as a colleague, student or instructor. I learned something every time I flew with you!

Instrument flying is when your mind gets a grip on the fact that there is vision beyond sight. —
U.S. Navy 'Approach' magazine, circa W.W.II

TABLE OF CONTENTS

When my friend, Pete Peterson was asked where he had learned to fly, he replied,
"I soloed in Show Low Arizona in 1935, and I've been learnin' ever since."

FAASafety.gov

 *Try to learn from the mistakes of others.*
You won't live long enough to make all of them by yourself.

Instrument Regulations

Staying IFR Current

Within the previous six calendar months, (the beginning of this six month window starts on the **1ˢᵗ**), you must have:

- o Completed an IPC, *or*
- o Maintained IFR currency by logging:
  - Six Instrument Approaches,
  - Holding procedures,
  - Course interceptions & tracking

Maintaining IFR currency can be accomplished:

- o In actual instrument conditions,
- o Hooded / Foggled with a safety pilot, *or*
- o In a simulator, under CFI-I supervision.
  - The CFI-I must sign your logbook, verifying that the simulated instrument time and approaches were accomplished. *(FAR 61.51)*

The simulator must be at least a desktop simulator, such as the *On Top Elite Basic ATD*.

The aircraft or simulator used for the IPC, or for maintaining IFR currency, is **category specific**. That is, you can't become or remain IFR current in a helicopter or helicopter simulator and expect that currency to be valid in an airplane.

Safety Pilots don't require an instrument rating, but must have:

- o A private pilot certificate with **category** and **class** ratings appropriate to the aircraft being flown, &
- o A current medical. *(FAR 91.109(b))*.

After the flight with a safety pilot, log the:

- Amount of simulated instrument time,
- Airport(s) where you flew the approaches,
- Types of instrument approaches, &
- Safety pilot's name.

Lost Currency

If you failed to fly six instrument approaches in the last six month window, you still have another six months – *a grace period* – to meet IFR currency requirements.

During the grace period, you can only dream of filing an IFR flight plan until, in simulated instrument conditions, you log enough approaches to bring the six month window total to six, plus holding, course interceptions and tracking.

If you fail to become current in the grace period, you'll need to take an IPC before filing an IFR flight plan.

IFR currency is child's play.

Doug Stewart, 2004 National Certificated Flight Instructor of the Year, and frequent contributor to **PilotWorkshops.com**, said this about maintaining instrument proficiency:

"I certainly highly recommend getting an IPC once every six months, even if you fly IFR once a week. It doesn't hurt to get another opinion; to get someone else to evaluate your IFR flying and your IFR skills. Obviously, if you aren't flying frequently, it behooves you all the more to do it."

2

PIC Responsibilities *(FAR 91.413)*

The PIC must make sure that his/her aircraft is airworthy. This includes ensuring that:

- The aircraft has received an Annual Inspection within the past 12 months. (The annual expires the last day of the 12th month). *(FAR 91.409)*
- The transponder has been tested and inspected within the past 24 months. (Expires the last day of the 24th month).

If filing IFR, ensure that the Pitot/Static System:

- Has been tested and inspected within the past 24 months. (Expires the last day of the 24th month).

VOR Checks *(FAR 91.171)*

Every 30 days, the VORs must be checked by using either of the following:

- VOR test signal (VOT), allowable difference $\pm 4°$.
- VOR ground check point, allowable difference $\pm 4°$.
- Designated airborne VOR checkpoint, allowable difference $+ 6°$.
  - The locations and details for VOTs, ground and airborne VOR checkpoints, can be found in the Airport Facility Directory (A/FD).
- Dual VOR checked against one another. The allowable difference is $\pm 4°$.
  - The VORs can be checked on the ground or in flight, but must be checked using the bearing "to" the station, &
  - The VOR receivers must be independent, except for the antennae.

Log the date, place and bearing error. In the case of a dual VOR check, record both bearings to the VOR.
Sign the log.

Drake VOR, 8-25-2011. #1 170°. #2 174°. Grant Canyon

Prescott VOT, 8-26-2011. #1 3°. #2 1°. Don Patrol

(FAR 91.171)

You may have your VORs tested at a repair station. The VORs must be $\pm 4°$ of the test signal and the repair station's technician must make an aircraft log entry, certifying the check.

Required Documents On Board *(FAR 91.203, 91.9)*
A-R-R-O-W

- o **A**irworthiness certificate,
- o **R**egistration certificate,
- o **R**adio license, (if traveling outside the USA, and for some commercial operations),
- o **O**perating limitations. (The Owner's Manual), &
- o **W**eight and balance data.

Required Personal Documents *(FAR 61.3)*

- o A current plastic (credit card style) pilot certificate that includes an "English Proficient" endorsement. (This endorsement is required for international flying),
- o An appropriate current medical, &
- o A government issued photo ID (Driver's license, military ID, or passport).

Misplaced License

Request temporary authority to exercise certificate privileges at *www.FAA.gov*. Sign into your account, and click on the *Licenses & Certificates* TAB. Select *"Airman Online Services"*.
The FAA will send a temporary certificate via fax or e-mail. You can only request one temporary certificate within any six-month period. While at *www.FAA.gov*, you can request a **replacement** certificate.

Changed Address *(FAR 61.60)*

The FAA must be notified within **30 days** of an address change, otherwise you may not act as pilot in command. You can change your address, add "English Proficient", or any other amendment to your status by logging on at *www.FAA.gov* and clicking on the *Licenses & Certificates* TAB.

You may also make address changes through the mail. The address is:

FAA
Airmen Certification Branch,
AFS-760
P.O. Box 25082
Oklahoma City, OK 73125-0082

IFR – Required Reports to ATC
With or Without RADAR Contact
(AIM 5-3-2, FAR 91-183)

- o Vacating an altitude.
- o Reaching a holding fix.
- o Leaving a holding fix.
- o VFR on top altitude change.
- o Missed approach with request for specific action.
- o TAS changes 10 knots or 5%, whichever is greater. (5% of 200 knots TAS is 10 knots).
- o Unable to maintain a 500 FPM climb.
- o Passing a point that ATC has asked you to report.
- o Safety of flight information.
- o Encountering un-forecasted weather.
- o Equipment malfunctions.
- o Malfunctions of navigation, approach, or communication equipment, and the degree to which the malfunction affects the pilot's ability to operate under IFR in the ATC system. Report the nature and extent of assistance needed from ATC. *(FAR 91.189)*

*AOPA's Air Safety Institute offers a course entitled "**IFR Insights: Regulations**"*

This course qualifies for Wings Credit and AOPA Accident Forgiveness.

IFR – Required Reports to ATC, IFR
Not in RADAR Contact:

- ○ **Non-Precision Approach:** Inbound, leaving FAF.
- ○ **Precision Approach:** Inbound, leaving an outer marker (OM) or the OM substitute.
- ○ The revised ETA is greater than three minutes.
- ○ When the estimated arrival time over a designated reporting point is off by more than three minutes.
- ○ Passing designated reporting points.

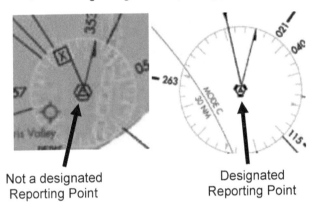

Not a designated   Designated
Reporting Point   Reporting Point

IFR Position Reports consist of:

- ○ Call sign,
- ○ Name of reporting point,
- ○ Time over reporting point,
- ○ Altitude,
- ○ "IFR". You can omit this if reporting to an approach or center controller. (They know that you're IFR),
- ○ Estimated time over the next reporting point, &
- ○ Name of the reporting point after the next reporting point.

Example: "Houston Center, N98X, over Junction at 2158, 10,000. Estimating Center Point at 2220. San Antonio next."

The worst day of flying still beats the best day of real work.

Transponders/Mode C

An operating Mode C is required in:

- Class A airspace,
- Class B airspace, (within 30 nm of the primary Class B airport),
- In <u>and above</u> Class C airspace, &
- Anytime, when operating above 10,000 MSL, (excluding the airspace below 2,500 AGL).

If your transponder fails in flight, ATC grant permission to continue to your destination.

The controller told me, "Radar contact lost", but my transponder's Reply Light is flashing. Why?

- Another radar, military or FAA, could be pinging the transponder, *or*
- The transponder may be responding to another aircraft's *Traffic Alert and Collision Avoidance System* (TCAS) interrogation.

Required Equipment

VFR Day (FAR 91.205)

- Fuel gauge for each tank.
- Oil Temp gauge for each <u>air cooled</u> engine.
- Oil Pressure gauge for each engine.
- Temp gauge for each <u>liquid cooled</u> engine.
- ELT *(FAR 91.207)*.
- Altimeter.
- Magnetic Compass.
- Airspeed Indicator.
- Tachometer for each engine.
- Manifold Pressure gauge for each *altitude engine*. (That's a turbocharged reciprocating engine, with boosted manifold pressure that must be monitored.)
- Landing gear position indicator, (if the aircraft has retractable gear).
- Anti-collision light system, if certified after March 11, 1996. (In the event of failure, you may continue to a location

where repair or replacement can be made.)
- o Seat Belts.
- o Shoulder straps – mandatory if the aircraft was manufactured after July, 1978.

More Seat Belt Requirements

Seat belts and shoulder straps, (if installed), are to be fastened during taxi, takeoff and landing. *(FAR 91.107).*
If a child is less than 24 months old, he or she can be held on a passenger's lap.

 ## Required Equipment

VRF Night *(FAR 91.205)*

- o Anti-collision light system, if the aircraft was certified after August 11, 1971. (In the event of failure, you may continue to a location where repair or replacement can be made.)
- o Position lights – ON from sunset to sunrise. *(Ref. FAR 91.209).*
- o Landing light, if flown for hire.
- o A power source.
- o Spare fuses – three of each kind required, and accessible in flight.

Required Equipment, IFR *(In addition to the equipment required for VFR)* *(FAR 91.205)*

- o Clock – Installed in the aircraft, displaying hours, minutes and seconds.
- o Directional Gyro.
- o Attitude Indicator.
- o Rate of turn indicator or an additional attitude indicator
- o Skid/Slip Indicator.
- o Two-way radios and navigational equipment appropriate to the ground facilities used.
- o Altimeter.
- o Generator or alternator with adequate capacity.

*You can take off with inoperative instruments or equipment that's not required by FAR 91, as long as that instrument or equipment is removed or placarded "**Inoperative**" and a pilot or mechanic determines that the loss of that instrument or equipment is not a hazard.*

Using a non-WAAS GPS for IFR Navigation

The aircraft must have installed and operational, all navigation equipment necessary to fly the route to the destination airport and any required alternate. All of the route's NAVAIDs must be operational.

WAAS GPS Benefits

CATEGORY	A	B	C	D
LPV DA	1608-1 250 (300-1)			
LNAV/VNAV DA	1685-1¼ 327 (400-1¼)			
LNAV MDA	1740-1 382 (400-1)			1740
CIRCLING	1800-1¼ 418 (500-1¼)	1840-1¼ 458 (500-1¼)	1840-1½ 458 (500-1½)	194

- o Pilots can use WAAS GPS as the primary navigation system from takeoff through landing, (No ground based NAVAIDs are required).
- o Pilots may fly RNAV/GPS approaches using "LNAV/VNAV", "LPV", or "LNAV" approach minimums.
- o Pilots can file for, and use, NAVAIDs that are NOTAMed out of service.

Substituting GPS for ADF and DME

(AIM 1-1-19 & 1-1-20)
An IFR GPS – either WAAS or non-WAAS – <u>usually</u> qualifies as a substitute for ADF and DME with the following exception:

- o If an approach is not a GPS overlay, such as an "**NDB or GPS**" approach, the aircraft must be equipped with an NDB to fly that approach.

IFR Fuel Requirements *(FAR 91.151 & 167)*

You'll need enough fuel to fly to the destination and the alternate (if required) + 45 minutes of reserve fuel.

Required Forecast Weather for a Legal Destination *(FAR 91.167)*

The destination weather must be forecast to be at or above that required for the planned approach.

You'll need an Alternate IF:

- o The destination doesn't have an instrument approach, *or*
- o One hour before and one hour after your planned arrival, the destination weather is forecast to be less than:
    - 2,000 ft ceiling, **or**
    - 3 statute miles visibility.

Memory Helper - The 1-2-3 Rule

- o ± *1* hour
- o **2**,000' ceiling
- o **3** miles visibility

If your destination does not have a Terminal Area Forecast (TAF), use the Area Forecast.

Alternate Weather Requirements *(FAR 91.167)*

- o Airports with a precision approach (ILS or PAR): **600 & 2.**
- o Airports with a non-precision approach – (no precision approach available): **800 & 2.**

Airports without an instrument approach can be used as an alternate if the forecast weather conditions are basic VFR from the Minimum Enroute Altitude (MEA) to the planned alternate airport.

MEA

WAAS GPS Alternate Planning – Exceptions (AIM 1-1-20)

Although LNAV/VNAV and LPV approach minimums approximate ILS approach minimums, they are still considered **non-precision approaches** (classified as an Approach with Vertical Guidance (APV)). Therefore, if an alternate doesn't have an ILS or PAR approach, it must have, ±1 hour of the ETA, a forecast of **800 & 2**.

WAAS & Non-WAAS GPS Approach Planning

o GPS users may plan to use a GPS-based instrument approach at either their destination or alternate airport, but not at both locations.

o Properly trained and approved WAAS GPS users, equipped with and using approved baro-VNAV equipment, may plan for LNAV/VNAV or RNP 0.3 DA at the alternate airport. (See page 102, Baro-VNAV).

o WAAS users **without Baro-VNAV** (that's most light GA aircraft users) may plan for an LNAV approach at an alternate airport.

IFR Operations to High Altitude Destinations and Alternates – Considerations (AIM 5-1-9)

Three high altitude airports in the U.S. have approved instrument approach procedures where all of the MDAs are greater than 2,000 feet and/or the landing visibility minimums are greater than 3 miles. These are South Lake Tahoe, CA (KTVL), Bishop, CA (KBIH) and Aspen, CO (KASE).

It is possible for a pilot to elect not to carry sufficient fuel to get to an alternate when the destination's forecast ceiling and/or visibility is actually lower than that necessary to complete the approach.

A small number of mountain airports have MDAs that are just below 2,000 feet AGL. If the weather deteriorates slightly, the airport could be below minimums.

	←—— 3.5 NM ——→	←—— 2.6 NM ——→	←——— 8.5 NM ———→	←—1 NM—→
CATEGORY	A	B	C	D
LNAV MDA	6600-1¼	6600-1½	6600-3	NA
	2477 (2500-1¼)	2477 (2500-1½)	2477 (2500-3)	
CIRCLING	6600-1¼	6600-1½	6600-3	NA
	2476 (2500-1¼)	2476 (2500-1½)	2476 (2500-3)	

EASTERN SIERRA RGNL (BIH)

37°22'N-118°22'W **RNAV (GPS) Y RWY 12**

Avionics Failures and Approaches

If an airport has approaches that require special equipment, such as DME or a glide slope, and the aircraft's DME or glide slope fails enroute, you may not be able to fly a successful approach.

Smart Alternate Shopping

- Avoid alternates within 10 minutes of your destination. They're in the same weather system.
- Pick a downwind alternate airport and if you need to go there, use best endurance power settings.
- Try to find an alternate with multiple approaches.
- Choose an alternate that isn't blocked by restricted or complicated airspace.
- Consider choosing a 2nd alternate that's prior to your destination, in case you need to cut your trip short.

When an Alternate is not an Alternate *(AIM 1-1-20)*

If the destination weather deteriorates, and you divert to your alternate, it's now your "**destination**" and the alternate weather requirements, (600 & 2, and 800 & 2), are replaced with the weather required to make the approach.

GPS users can <u>plan</u> to use a GPS-based instrument approach at either their destination or alternate airport, <u>but not at both locations</u>. After diverting to an alternate, any approach is fair game.

GPS & RAIM *(Receiver Autonomous Integrity Monitoring)* *(AIM 1-1-19)*

The GPS receiver verifies the integrity or usability of the constellation of GPS satellite signals to determine if a satellite is providing corrupt info. A RAIM failure annunciates **two minutes** after the GPS can't see at least **5** satellites for integrity monitoring, or **two minutes after** the RAIM integrity monitor detects a potential error.

RAIM Warnings on Approach

- If a RAIM failure annunciates prior to the final approach waypoint (FAWP) – Execute a missed approach.
- If a RAIM failure annunciates after passing the FAWP – The receiver may continue to operate and allow you to complete the approach without a warning. If a warning appears – Execute a missed approach.

PREDICTING GPS RAIM, Non-WAAS GPS

Non-WAAS GPS users must confirm GPS RAIM availability prior to an IFR flight. Checking *http://sapt.faa.gov/default.php* satisfies this requirement. If you flight plan using FltPlan.com, it will automatically check RAIM for you.   ✓ **GPS RAIM**

Wide Area Augmentation System (WAAS) NOTAMs

GPS NOTAMs can be located online at
https://pilotweb.nas.faa.gov/PilotWeb/

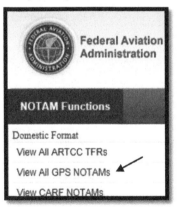

Enter a location. Then, from the *"NOTAM Functions"* menu, select *"View All GPS NOTAMs"*

SAMPLE WAAS NOTAM:
!BOS BOS WAAS LPV AND LNAV/VNAV MNM UNREL WEF 0305231700—0305231815.

In a WAAS NOTAM, the term *"UNREL"* means that the expected level of WAAS service may not be available.

WAAS NOTAMs are Predictive and things could change. For instance, using the sample WAAS NOTAM above: If upon arrival in BOS, it appears that the LNAV/VNAV or LPV service is available, (annunciated as such on the GPS), vertical guidance to LNAV/VNAV or LPV minimums is allowed.

If a WAAS NOTAM has not been included in the ATIS broadcast, controllers are required to tell pilots about the NOTAM as they clear him or her for a RNAV (GPS) approach.

Negative "W" (No WAAS NOTAMs Symbol)

Airports that are on the edge of WAAS coverage may experience WAAS vertical guidance outages on a daily basis. At those airports, a negative **W** symbol appears on their RNAV (GPS) approach charts, meaning that WAAS NOTAMs **are not provided**.

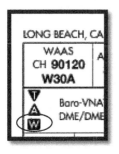

At these airports, whether used for a destination or alternate, plan to use LNAV minimums. Upon arrival, if WAAS GPS annunciations indicate LNAV/VNAV or LPV, you may use the lower WAAS minimums. Be prepared to revert to the higher "LNAV" minimums if a WAAS outage occurs.

 Why can't I use my hand held WAAS enabled GPS for IFR approaches?

Hand held GPS units lack RAIM checking, CDI/HIS connectivity and the installation planning of a panel mounted GPS.

FL180 and Above – Class A Airspace

In Class airspace:

o   You must be on an IFR flight plan. No VFR on Top allowed.
o   A transponder is required.
o   You must set your altimeter to 29.92 when climbing through the transition level – usually 18,000 feet MSL.
o   The assigned altitudes are called "Flight Levels". FL180, FL190, etc.
o   Above FL240, DME is required.
o   FL 180 is not usable when the altimeter setting is below 29.92, but higher than 28.92. In this case, the lowest assignable flight level is FL190. (*See FAR 91.121 for more information*)

Weather Reports and Forecasts

Many pilots get a synopsis of the weather from morning TV shows and *The Weather Channel*. Although not FAA approved weather briefing sources, they provide an overall outlook, and help in your planning a day or two before the flight.

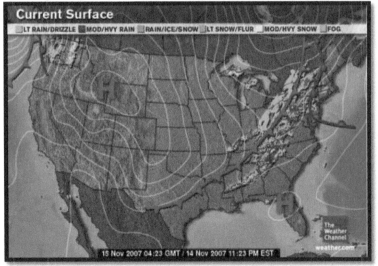

Approved briefing sources, such as a Flight Service briefer and DUAT / DUATS, utilize Area Forecasts, Terminal Forecasts (TAF), Terminal weather reports (METARS), PIREPS, Radar pictures, Winds aloft forecasts, AIRMETS, SIGMETS, and Convective SIGMETS.

"Everybody talks about the weather, but nobody does anything about it."
Mark Twain

Internet Weather Sources

http://aviationweather.gov

Both **DUATS** and **DUAT** are under contract with the FAA to provide authorized weather briefings, and they certify to the FAA that you have received a weather and airspace briefing, and assumes that you actually read the online briefing.

This is a QICP (Qualified Internet Communications Provider) weather service; an FAA approved and certified source of Weather and NOTAMS. However, unlike DUATS and DUAT, it does not certify to the FAA that you have received a weather/airspace briefing.

16

Weather Reports

The term **METAR** comes from the French phrase, *"message d'observation mét*éorologique pour l'*a*viation *r*égulière" *METARs are Reported using:*

o Visibility – Statute miles.
o Cloud Heights – AGL.
o Wind Direction – True.
o Wind Speeds – Knots

METAR Example

METAR KLGA 051853Z 04011KT 1/2SM VCTS SN FZFG BKN003 OVC010 M02/M02 A3006 RMK AO2 TSB40 SLP176 P0002 T10171017=

METAR Example Decoded

KLGA – weather from LaGuardia, NY

051853Z indicates the day of the month is the **5th** and the time of day is **1853** Zulu time.

04011KT indicates the wind direction and speed – **040 at 11 knots**.

1/2SM indicates the prevailing visibility is ½ statute mile.

VCTS indicates there is a thunderstorm in the **vicinity**, (within 10SM, but beyond 5SM).

SN indicates **snow** is falling at a moderate intensity.

FZFG indicates the presence of **freezing fog**.

BKN003 indicates a **broken** cloud layer at **300 feet AGL**.

OVC010 indicates an **overcast** cloud layer at **1,000 feet AGL**.

M02/M02 indicates the temperature is **minus 2° Celsius** and the dew point is **minus 2°** Celsius.

A3006 indicates the altimeter setting is **30.06**

RMK indicates the **remarks section follows**.

AO2 indicates that the station has an **automated precipitation sensor**.

TSB40 indicates the **thunderstorm began 40 minutes after the top of the hour at 1840 Zulu time.**

SLP176 indicates the current barometric pressure extrapolated to sea level is **1017.6 millibars**

P0002 indicates that **0.02 of precipitation** accumulated during the last hour.

T10171017 indicates the temperature is 29°F, (converted to minus 1.7° Celsius), and the dew point is 29°F, (converted to minus 1.7° Celsius).

= indicates the **end** of the METAR report.

All the METARs in the United States are graphically displayed on the "Weather Depiction Chart"

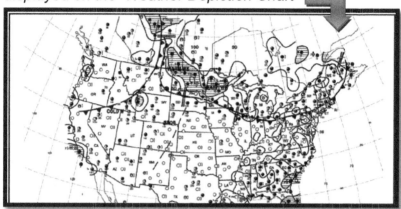

Weather Depiction Chart Symbols

Few clouds (no cloud height is given for "few".

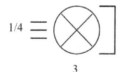

Total obscuration. Vertical vis: 300 feet. ¼ mile fog. The bracket to the right indicates that the report is from an automated system.

Scattered clouds at 2,500 ASL.

Scattered clouds at 3,000 AGL with 5 miles visibility and haze.

Broken clouds at 2,000 AGL with 3 miles visibility and continuous rain.

 Overcast clouds at 500 AGL with 1 mile visibility and intermittent snow.

5

 Broken clouds at 1000 AGL with 1 ½ mile visibility and there is also a thunderstorm with rain shower.

 Missing cloud cover or partial obscuration.

Weather Depiction Charts show:

- IFR areas, depicted by shading inside the contours.
- Marginal VFR (MVFR), depicted by contours without shading.
- Good VFR weather, depicted outside the contours.

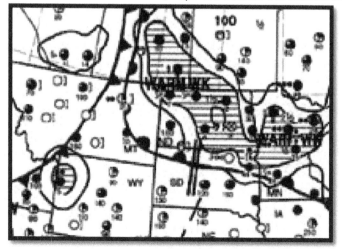

Forecasts

Area Forecasts are issued three times a day and are made up of several sections of the continental US, the Gulf of Mexico, Alaska, Hawaii, and the Caribbean. With a wide area forecast, you can determine the forecast Enroute weather, and interpolate weather conditions at airports that don't have a terminal forecast (TAF).

Area Forecasts report:

o Cloud tops – MSL.
o Times – UTC.
o Winds – Knots.
o Wind Direction –True.
o Distances – Nautical.
o Visibility – Statute.

Area Forecast Example

KANSAS
Western...SCT080 scattered cirrus. Wind southeast G25KT. Outlook: VFR 5:00 MVFR ceiling Mist.
Central...SCT080-100 scattered cirrus. Until 16:00 extreme southern occasional BKN100 top 160. Outlook: VFR 3:00 MVFR ceiling mist.
Eastern...broken-SCT060 top 120 scattered-broken cirrus. Becoming 17:00 to 19:00 SCT040 broken-SCT080 Top 160. Outlook: VFR 2:00 northeastern MVFR ceiling mist.

Terminal Airdrome Forecasts (TAFs) predict weather within a 5 mile radius of the airport.

The trouble with weather forecasting is that it's right too often for us to ignore it and for us to ignore it and wrong too often for us to rely on it. – Patrick Young

20

TAF Example

KXYZ 241732Z **2418/2524** 11006KT 4SM -SHRA BKN030
FM242300 22006KT 3SM -SHRA OVC030
PROB30 2504/2506 VRB20G35KT 1SM +TSRA BKN015CB

FM 250600 250010KT 4SM -SHRA OVC050
TEMPO 2508/2511 2SM -SHRA OVC030=

TAF Example Decoded

2418/25: Indicates the valid time of the 30-hour TAF, where 2418 is the 24th day at 1800 UTC, and 2524 is the 25th day at 2400 UTC, (or 0000 UTC on the 26th).

FM242300: Indicates a significant and rapid change to a new set of prevailing conditions, in this case starting at 2300 UTC on the 24th.

PROB30: Indicates the probability of the occurrence of a thunderstorm or other precipitation event. In this case, occurring during the two-hour period between **0400 UTC and 0600 UTC on the 25th.**

TEMPO 2508/2511: Indicates a temporary fluctuation in forecast conditions. In this case, during the two-hour period between 0800 UTC and 0011 UTC on the 25th

Winds aloft reports are of incomparable value –
to historians.

Winds Aloft Forecasts *are reported in True North. By studying Winds Aloft, you can discover:*

- o Temperature inversions.
- o The most favorable cruising altitude.
- o Areas of possible icing, (temps +2° to –20° C).

Abrupt changes in wind direction and speed at different altitudes could indicate the possibility of turbulence.

```
000
FDUW01 KWBC 110159
DATA BASED ON 110000Z
VALID 110600Z    FOR USE 0500-0900Z. TEMPS NEG ABV 24000

FT   3000    6000    9000   12000   18000   24000   30000   34
PHX 2712 2916+08 3015-01 2913-08 3030-21 3236-34 304642 285
PRC              3113-01 3016-08 3225-21 3443-34 335144 313
TUS         3115+07 2714-01 2617-06 2839-18 2759-31 257638 268
ALS                      1714+00 1758-16 1960-30 198843 207
DEN              0214+01 0708-04 1532-15 1744-27 205743 206
GJT              0509+01 0505-07 1722-20 1755-32 166848 184
PUB              9900+11 1817+02 1841-16 2056-29 207142 205
BOI         3605+10 9900+02 9900-06 3611-19 3522-30 353446 343
```

Winds Aloft Example Decoded

- o Over DEN at 12,000 feet, the wind is from 070° at 8 knots; temp -4°C.
- o Winds are not forecast for levels less than 1,500 feet above a station. For instance the high stations such as PRC, DEN, GJT and PUB don't forecast winds until 9,000 feet, and ALS forecasts start at 12,000 feet.
- o Over GJT at 18,000 feet, the wind is from 170° at 22 knots; -20° C.
- o Over BOI at 9,000 feet, **"9900"** = Wind is light and variable.
- o **7510-41** – The **seven** indicates winds over 100 knots. (Subtract 5 from first number and insert a 1 in front of the 3rd number) = Wind from 250° @ 110knots; temp is -41° C
- o At and above 30,000 feet, the minus sign is not used; assume a negative temperature.

Convective Outlook

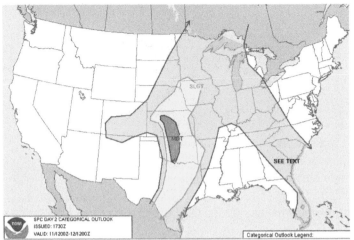

A Convective Outlook is issued five times daily, and forecasts the chances of thunderstorms as either:

- ○ General (shaded areas which are not labeled),
- ○ Slight (Labeled SLGT)
- ○ Moderate (Labeled MDT), or
- ○ High

SIGMETs (SIGnificant Meteorological Information)

Convective SIGMETs predict thunderstorms and imply severe icing potential. They are issued every hour at 55 minutes past the hour in the continental US. If no convective SIGMET is forecast, "CONVECTIVE SIGMET NONE" is issued. They are valid a maximum of two hours. *Convective SIGMETs include:*

- ○ Lines or areas of thunderstorms covering 40% or more of a 3,000 square mile or larger area.
- ○ Embedded thunderstorms (obscured) and severe thunderstorms if they are expected to endure more than 30 minutes. Severe thunderstorms include tornadoes, thunderstorms, hail, and wind gusts greater or equal to 50 knots.

23

SIGMETs warn of significant <u>non-convective</u> weather that's hazardous to all aircraft. SIGMETs may be issued at any time, and have a maximum forecast period of 4 hours.

SIGMETs are issued for:

- Severe icing
- Severe turbulence
- Clear air turbulence
- Sand and dust storms
- Volcanic ash (valid up to six hours)
- Large areas of IFR conditions and possible mountain obscuration
- Sustained surface winds greater or equal to 30 knots

In Alaska and Hawaii, SIGMETs are also issued for tornadoes, a line of thunderstorms, embedded thunderstorms, or hail greater than or equal to 3/4 inch

AIRMETs - (AIRman's METeorological Information)

These warn pilots of weather that's potentially hazardous to all aircraft, but doesn't meet the criteria for a SIGMET.

AIRMETs are widespread, affecting an area of at least 3,000 square miles at any one time. That's the combined size of Rhode Island and Delaware.

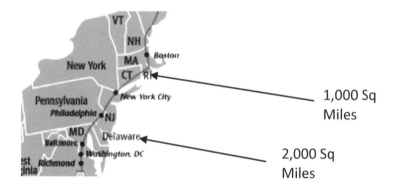

An **AIRMET** is a "time smeared forecast" that's valid for a six hour period. If the total area to be affected during the forecast period is very large, it could be that only a small portion of the total area would be affected at any one time.

AIRMETs are issued for:

- **Instrument Flight Rules (IFR),** meaning:
  - Ceilings less than 1000 feet and/or visibility less than 3 miles affecting over 50% of the area at one time, &
  - Extensive mountain obscuration.
- **Turbulence,** including:
  - Moderate Turbulence, &
  - Sustained surface winds of greater than 30 knots on the surface
- **Icing,** including:
  - Moderate icing, &
  - The freezing levels

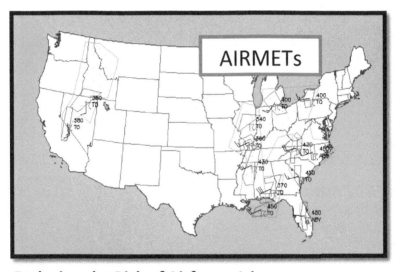

Reducing the Risk of Airframe Icing

Avoid freezing rain (FZRA) and freezing drizzle (FZDZ). Convective SIGMETs imply severe icing potential. A 50% relative humidity may imply a high probability of icing.

As you get closer to the center of a low pressure system, moisture moves upwards faster, resulting in icing conditions at higher altitudes.
Look for amended TAFs & obtain PIREPs for the route.

Ice Bridging

At the first indication of wing ice, cycle the boots unless the aircraft's manual specifically prohibits this.

The NTSB has found that *Ice Bridging* is extremely rare because de-icing boots are now modified to effectively remove ice without waiting for a substantial ice buildup. The NTSB recommends that you cycling the de-icing boots continuously while in icing conditions. Turn the autopilot off so you can feel handling changes. *(Ref. NTSB Safety Alert, SA-014, Dec 2008).*

THE RISK OF ICING			
RISK ⬇	**CUMULUS CLOUDS**	**STRATIFORM CLOUDS**	**RAIN & DRIZZLE**
HIGH	0° C TO - 20°C	0°C TO - 15°C	0°C & BELOW
MEDIUM	-20°C TO - 40°C	-15°C TO - 30°C	
LOW	LESS THAN - 40°C	LESS THAN - 32°C	

No Ice Protection

If you don't have an ice removal / prevention system, then you must seek warmer air. How warm? At 3°C, the ice will slowly dissipate. At 4°C or more, the ice will rapidly melt.

Photo Courtesy of NASA Glenn

Freezing Rain

When encountering freezing rain, if you climb, you might find warmer air. That's because freezing rain requires a temperature inversion.

On Jan 2009, the FAA declared that each encounter with ice will be judged by whether a "reasonable and prudent" pilot would take the same actions or make the same decisions as the pilot in the icing situation.

Current Icing Potential and Forecast Icing Potential (CIP/FIP)

See: WWW.*AviationWeather.gov*
(Click on *"SIGMET/AIRMET"*, and then the *"Icing"* Tab).

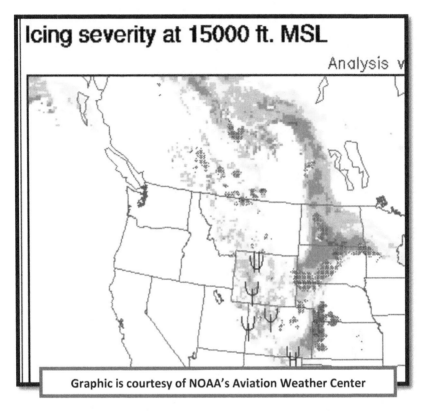

Icing severity at 15000 ft. MSL

Analysis

Graphic is courtesy of NOAA's Aviation Weather Center

CIP/FIP is not meant to be a "stand alone" chart, and must be used with AIRMET / SIGMET Icing, and ceiling / temp charts to enhance awareness. Although very useful for forecasting the potential for icing, **the CIP / FIP charts are not reliable when trying to forecast where icing will NOT exist.**

Super Cooled Liquid Droplet (SLD) forecasts are included in the CIP/FIP chart (marked in red). SLDs are up to 100 times the size of other ice droplets. Even with de-icing protection, SLDs are very dangerous and should be avoided.

Ice Reports are based on the rate of accumulation

- ○ **Trace** – accumulates slightly greater than sublimation. (Deicing might be used after an hour or more).
- ○ **Light** – might be a problem if flight is prolonged over an hour. (Need the occasional use of deicing equipment).
- ○ **Moderate** – means that short encounters are potentially hazardous. (<u>Must</u> use deicing equipment or divert).
- ○ **Severe** – the deicing equipment fails to reduce or control the icing. (Immediate diversion is necessary).

Where does ice collect first?
Small and/or narrow objects like the OAT probe present the first indication of icing.

Where is ice most dangerous?
The propeller and tail plane are thinner and could gather ice before it's noticed on the wings. An iced tailplane can stall first, forcing a nose down attitude when you lower the flaps or start to flare. If you suspect icing, use flaps judiciously, if at all.

Tail Plane Stalls
Pilots can't see the tail plane to determine if it's iced. To complicate matters, the tail plane stall recovery procedure is completely opposite of the wing stall recovery. Fighting against the way a pilot has been trained, puts him or her in very dangerous territory.

*NASA offers two courses, "**A Pilot's Guide to In-flight Icing**" and "**A Pilot's Guide to Ground Icing**" at:*

http://aircrafticing.grc.nasa.gov/ courses.html

*AOPA's Air Safety Institute (ASI) offers several weather interactive courses in their "**Weather Wise**" series, covering Thunderstorms and ATC, Precipitation and Icing, Air Masses and Fronts, and Ceilings and Visibility.* These courses qualify for Wings Credit and AOPA Accident Forgiveness.

*In addition, AOPA's ASI offers "**Accident Case Study: Airframe Icing**".* This course qualifies for AOPA Accident Forgiveness.

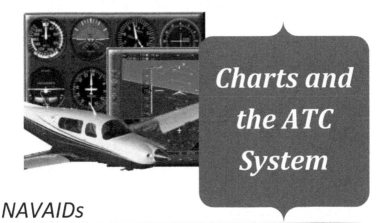

NAVAIDs

VOR STANDARD SERVICE VOLUME	ALTITUDE AND RANGE BOUNDARIES
T (Terminal)	From 1,000' AGL up to 12,000' AGL; 25 nm radius
L (Low Altitude)	From 1,000' AGL up to 18,000' AGL; 40 nm radius. Used only on Victor airways
H (High Altitude)	From 1,000' AGL to 14,500' AGL; 40 nm radius From 14,500 AGL to 60,000'; 100 nm radius Used on Victor airways and Jet routes.

Some Victor airways have MEAs that seem to be too low for the VOR's service volume and altitude / range boundaries. However, these MEAs have been flight tested and proven to provide good VOR reception.

NDB SERVICE VOLUMES & CLASS

CLASS NDB	Wattage	Effective Range
Compass Locator 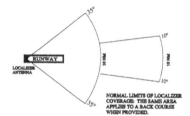 Outer marker, Middle maker, Inner marker, Compass locator	Below 25	**15 nm**
MH	Below 5	**25 nm**
H	50 to 1,999	**50 nm**
HH	2,000+	**75 nm**

MARKER BEACONS

Type	Where one would encounter it:
OM	Intercepting the ILS Glide slope
MM	3,500' from the landing threshold (at 200' above the touchdown zone)
IM	At Decision Height (DH)

(Reference AIM 1)

Localizer Coverage Limits / LOC BC & GS

Localizers offer course guidance up to 18 nm from the antenna.

ATC and the IFR Chart Review

Victor airways

- Class E airspace.
- 1,200 feet AGL to 18,000 feet MSL.
- Generally, the width is 4 nm either side of the airway, expanding to 4.5 nm, 102+ nm from each VOR.

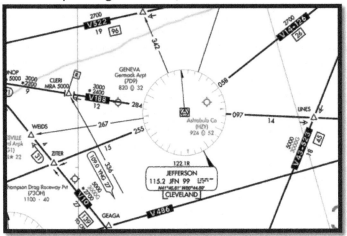

Jet routes – 18,000 feet MSL to 45,000 feet MSL.

Above 45,000 feet, aircraft use GPS or other navigational systems to fly their own points – direct, and off the airways.

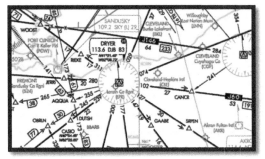

Colored routes

- o NDB radials with color prefixes – "Red", Green", "Amber", and "Blue", followed by a number, such as R4, G16, A7, B2, etc.
- o Found along the Carolina coastal waters, and in Alaska.

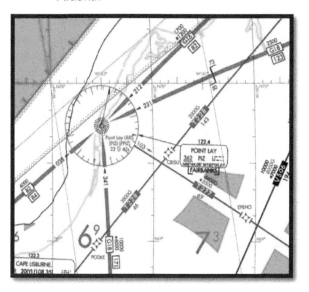

GPS/RNAV Airways

- o Depicted in blue
- o "T" prefix on the Lo Charts
- o "Q" prefix on the Hi Charts

"Tango" or "T" routes

- o "Terminal" routes exist below the ARTCC airspace.
- o Used by RNAV equipped aircraft from 1,200 feet above the surface, (or in some instances higher), and up to but not including 18,000 feet MSL.

Q – routes

- ○ Depicted on Enroute **High** Altitude Charts
- ○ Used by RNAV equipped aircraft between 18,000 feet MSL and FL 450 inclusive.

MEA – **M**inimum **E**n route **A**ltitude –

- ○ Assures acceptable navigational signal coverage
- ○ Meets obstacle clearance requirements between VORs
    - 1,000 feet or greater clearance in non-mountainous areas
    - Greater than 2,000 feet clearance in mountainous areas.

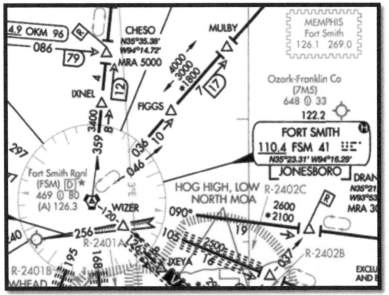

GPS MEAs – "G" suffix.

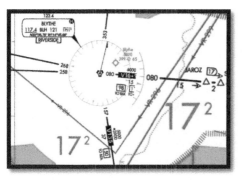

OROCA – **O**ff

Route **O**bstruction

Clearance **A**ltitude

- o Found in each quadrangle of an IFR Chart,
- o 1,000 foot obstacle clearance in non-mountainous terrain
- o 2,000 foot obstacle clearance in mountainous terrain.
- o Used for off-airway navigation.

If at the OROCA, you may not:

- o Be able to receive ground-based NAVAID signals,
- o Be high enough to be seen by air traffic control radar,
- o Be able to communicate with air traffic control.

It is far better to arrive late in this world than early in the next.

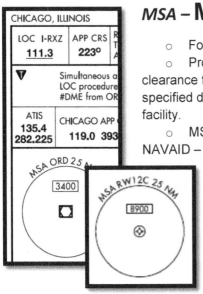

MSA – **M**inimum **S**afe **A**ltitudes

- o Found on approach plates.
- o Provide 1,000 feet obstacle clearance for emergency use within a specified distance from the listed navigation facility.
- o MSA is normally based on the NAVAID – VORTAC or NDB:
    - o RNAV straight-in approach MSAs are based on the runway waypoint (RWY WP).
    - o RNAV circling approach MSAs are based on the airport waypoint (APT WP).
- o GPS approach MSAs are based on the missed approach waypoint (MAWP), such as the runway threshold.

MAA – **M**aximum **A**uthorized **A**ltitudes

- o Maximum altitude limits for a route.
- o Above the MAA, it could be possible to tune in a faraway station that has the same frequency, but has nothing to do with the airway.
- o GPS routes like T207 and T204, (shown above), don't involve VORs, but an MAA is most likely depicted because a higher altitude may interfere with Center's airspace.

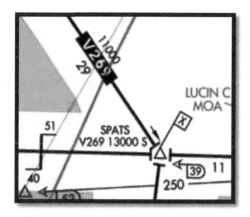

MCA – **M**inimum **C**rossing **A**ltitude
A fix or NAVAID that must be <u>crossed</u> at or above a required altitude.

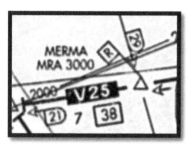

MRA – **M**inimum **R**eception **A**ltitude

o Lowest altitude at which an intersection can be determined with two VORs.
o Provides terrain clearance.

COP – **C**hange **O**ver **P**oint
The point at which you must switch from one VOR to another.

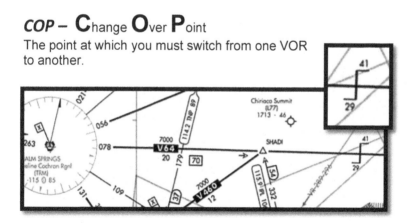

MOCA – **M**inimum **O**bstacle **C**learance **A**ltitudes

- o   *Jeppesen's* MOCA depiction: **1000T**.
- o   *AeroNav (formerly NACO)* chart depiction: ***1000**.
- o   Provides terrain clearance and NAVAID reception within 22 nautical miles of the NAVAID.
- o   If both an MEA and MOCA are listed on the airway, the pilot can fly as low as the MOCA, (with ATC clearance, of course), if he or she is within 22 nm of the VOR concerned. *(FAR 91.177)*

Minimum Vectoring Altitude (MVA) is the lowest MSL

altitude at which an IFR aircraft will be vectored by a radar controller. The vectoring altitudes for radar approaches, departures, and missed approaches could be lower.

MVAs meet IFR obstacle-clearance criteria –

- o   *Non-Mountainous Areas:* 1,000 feet above the highest obstacle.
- o   *Mountainous Areas:* 2,000 feet above the highest obstacle.
  - •   1,000 foot clearance above the highest obstacle may be authorized with the use of Airport Surveillance Radar (ASR).

The MVA may be lower than the published MEA along an airway or jet-route segment, and can be used for radar vectoring if the controller has an adequate radar return.

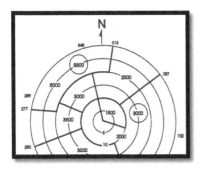

Charts depicting MVAs are available only for the controllers.

MVAs and Terrain Clearance Responsibility

If a controller makes a mistake and vectors you into terrain, he might bear some responsibility, but you're still dead. *Maintain situational awareness and:*

- o Use the VFR Charts and all available NAVAIDs to crosscheck terrain clearance altitudes.
- o If in doubt, query the controller.
- o If you have Ground Proximity Warning / Terrain Warning, utilize and respect it!

RNAV / GPS Direct Flight Planning

Graphic courtesy of Garmin

- o Avoid all sensitive areas such as TFRs, Restricted, and Prohibited areas.
- o Your route should include one "real fix" – a fix that ATC will recognize – in each ARTCC area.
- o ATC requires radar coverage and monitoring for a direct flight.

Unpublished RNAV Routes are direct routes based on area navigation / GPS capability between waypoints defined by:

- o Latitude/longitude, *or*
- o Degree-distance fixes, *or*
- o Offsets from established airways at a specified distance and direction.

All unpublished RNAV routes require ATC radar monitoring.

ATC's Preferred IFR Routes are found in the A/FD and are divided into low or high altitude routes. These can be one way or two way routes.

Tower Enroute Control (TEC) – See A/FD

It is possible to fly IFR from one airport to another without leaving approach control's airspace – flying beneath the "Enroute" structure. Here's an example from the A/FD:

FROM: SNA **TO:** CRQ NFG NKX OKB   **ROUTE ID:** CSTN30
ROUTE: V23 OCN   **ALTITUDE:** PQ50 (5,000 feet)

AIRCRAFT CLASSIFICATION:

- ○ (J) = Jet powered
- ○ (M) Turbo Props/ Special (cruise speed 190 knots or greater)
- ○ (P) Non-jet (cruise speed 190 knots or greater
- ○ (Q) Non-jet (cruise speed 189 knots or less

AOPA's Air Safety Institute offers a course entitled "IFR Insights: Charts"

This course qualifies for Wings Credit and AOPA Accident Forgiveness.

39

The way I see it, you can either work for a living or you can fly airplanes. Me, I'd rather fly.

— Len Morgan

Forget all that stuff about thrust and drag, lift and gravity. An airplane flies because of money.

Instruments and Their Role

Pitch Instruments *(outlined in white)*

Airspeed, attitude, altimeter, and VVI/VSI.

Bank Instruments *(outlined in white)*

Turn and bank, attitude, and heading

Power Instruments

Airspeed + engine power instruments

Turn Rates

A standard rate turn:

- o Turns at 3° per second,
- o Requires 2 minutes to turn 360°.
- o Air traffic controllers assume that pilots will make standard rate turns, up to, but not exceeding 30° of bank.

o Faster airspeeds require more bank angle to achieve a standard rate turn.

- • 100 knots, requires about 15° bank angle.
- • 300 knots, requires about 40° bank angle.

Mag Compass Turning Errors

Undershoot North,
Overshoot SOUTH

o **UN** - When turning to the NORTH, the magnetic compass UNDERSHOOTS. Rollout BEFORE the desired heading. If turning from a NORTHERLY heading, the compass LAGs, and actually starts a turn in the opposite direction.

o **OS** - When turning to the SOUTH, the compass OVERSHOOTS. Rollout PAST the desired heading. If turning from a SOUTHERLY heading, the compass LEADs, and starts a turn more rapidly in the correct direction.

Limiting the bank to standard rate or less, limits the errors.

Sometimes the Mag Compass is Almost Perfect

When turning to an EAST or WEST heading, there's no lagging or leading. Roll out on the desired heading.

Acceleration and Deceleration Errors

Accelerate **N**orth, **D**ecelerate **S**outh

- **AN** - If flying EASTERLY or WESTERLY, and the airspeed is **ACCELERATING,** the compass will indicate a turn to the **NORTH**.

- **DS** - If flying EASTERLY or WESTERLY, and the airspeed is **DECELERATING,** the compass will indicate a turn to the **SOUTH**.

Mag Dip causes compass errors when turning, accelerating, and decelerating.

- The rollout correction for Northerly and Southerly turns is approximately equal to the latitude.
- If in the southern half of the United States, use 30° as a rollout correction.
- If in the northern half of the United States, use 40°.

ADF

Fixed Card ADF – all numbers are *relative* to the aircraft's magnetic heading.
For instance:
If heading 345°, and the ADF indicator shows the beacon at 75° relative to the aircraft's heading, the beacon is to the right, so
ADD:

- 345° + 75° = 420.
- Subtract 360 from 420 and that equals 060.
- The magnetic bearing to the beacon is 060°.

If heading 345° and the ADF indicator shows the beacon at 300° relative to the aircraft heading or 60° to the left, then you should **SUBTRACT:**

- 345° − 60° = 285°.
- The magnetic bearing to the beacon is 285°

ADF Bearing Interception

- Determine the angle between the head of the needle and the nose or tail of the aircraft.
- Double that angle up to 90° to select the intercept heading.
- When the intercept angle equals the angle between the needle and the nose or tail of the airplane, you have intercepted the course.

If off course and tracking inbound: Turn TOWARDS the head of the needle, plus an appropriate correction to return to the desired course.

If off course and tracking OUTBOUND: Turn AWAY from the tail of the needle, plus an appropriate correction to return to the desired on course.

Flying is the second greatest thrill known to man.... Landing is the first!

"That's what we're trained to do." — Chesley B. 'Sully' Sullenberger III, Captain of US Airways flight 1549.

The A320 ditched in the Hudson River with no loss of life. The New York Times reported on 16 January 2009 that he "had just performed a remarkable feat of flying. Some were calling it a miracle. But there he stood, calmly, inside the glass waiting room at the New York Waterway terminal on Pier 79, speaking to police officials. His fine gray hair was unruffled, and his navy blue pilot's uniform had barely a wrinkle." 15 January 2009.

NOTAMs & Before Takeoff

The FAA posts NOTAMS at
www.faa.gov/pilots/flt_plan/notams/

Distant (D) NOTAMs include time
critical information that might affect safety, such as:

- ○ Airport closure
- ○ Inoperative navigational

Key words within the first part of the NOTAM's text specify the area of concern:

- ○ RWY (Runway)
- ○ TWY (Taxiway)
- ○ SVC (Services

D NOTAM examples:

- ○ LAX NAV RWY 24R ILS OTS WEF 1106132100-1106132300
- ○ LAX TWY C CLSD BTN TWY P,C12 WEF 1106111400-1106131400
- ○ CDC 01/044 DXZ RWY 19 MALSR CMSN
- ○ LAX 06/046 LAX OBST CRANE 286 MSL (AGL UNKN) 3300 WSW RWY 24L FLAGGED AND LGTD

*NOTAM Changes: UAR NOTAMs, and USD NOTAMs, (applying to departure and arrival procedures), previously listed in the Airspace NOTAMS section, are now in the **FDC NOTAMs** section, with keywords of SID, ODP and STARS.*

FDC NOTAMS (Flight Data Center) are regulatory and concern:

- ○ Standard instrument departures (SIDs)
- ○ Graphic obstacle clearance departures (ODPs)
- ○ Standard terminal arrivals (STARs)
- ○ Airspace usage
- ○ TFRs and permanently closed airports

FDC NOTAM example:

FDC **1/3124** (KLAX A1338/11) LAX FI/T SID LOS ANGELES INTL, LOS ANGELES, CA. GABRE SIX DEPARTURE ROUTE DESCRIPTION: EXPECT ATC CLEARANCE AT 12,000.

GPS NOTAMs can be located online at:

https://pilotweb.nas.faa.gov/PilotWeb/
From the "*NOTAM Functions*" menu, select "*View All GPS NOTAMs*"

GPS NOTAM Example:
GPS **05/016** (KNMH A0037/11) GPS NAV PRN 30 OTS

IFR Proposed Departure Time

If your flight plan hasn't been activated by the proposed departure time plus one hour, your flight plan will most likely be deleted from the system. To ensure that your flight plan remains active, notify ATC or FSS of your revised departure time.

To receive an IFR clearance at an uncontrolled airport, call FSS for an IFR clearance, or the airport's approach control frequency. If those options are not available, call IFR Clearance Delivery at **888.766.8267, or 888-SPOT-BOT**.

If you do not depart by the void time specified in your clearance, you must notify ATC as soon as possible, but not more than 30 minutes after the void time. ATC initiates search and rescue 30 minutes after void time.

GPS Preflight

Verify that you have a current GPS database.

Before Engine Start

When the electric turn indicator is powered, and before starting the engine, listen for unusual noises as the gyro spins. (Problem noises will not be heard once the engine starts.)

Before Takeoff Checks

- o   VORs – Check.
- o   Altimeter should be ± 75 feet of field elevation.
- o   VSI – Zero, or note the error.
- o   Attitude Indicator – Set
- o   Heading Indicator – Set before taxi.

After starting the engine, the gyro driven attitude and heading indicators may not reach operating speed for five minutes.

Taxi Check

- o   Check the brakes
  - o   Ensure that the turn coordinator indicates turns and the ball moves to the outside of the turns.

The attitude indicator should erect and remain level within five minutes of engine start. If it's not level during taxi, or tilts more than 5 degrees during taxi turns – the attitude indicator is NOT reliable.

Heading Indicator Precession

In flight, precession should be no more than 3° every 15 minutes.

Mistakes are inevitable in aviation, especially when one is still learning new things. The trick is to not make the mistake that will kill you. —
Stephen Coonts

Clearance

It's always given in the same sequence – **C-R-A-F-T**:

Clearance limit – Route – Altitude – Frequency

(Departure) – Transponder Code

Caffeine Clearance Delivery

Have you ever tried to copy an IFR clearance and the controller – having had one too many cups of coffee – is talking much faster than you can listen and write?
 Well, forget about what you missed and just continue to write. Perhaps you missed the route, but you can write down the altitude, departure frequency and the squawk code.

You now have most of the clearance, and you could then read back, "Cessna 123XZ is cleared to San Antonio via direct EDWAR, **rest of the route missing**, climb and maintain 4,000, expect 10,000, ten minutes after departure, departure frequency . . . ", and so forth.

The controller can now reply with, "The rest of the route from EDWAR is Victor 68, Junction, V198, San Antonio."
That saves a lot of time and un-clutters the frequency. So, don't focus on what you missed. Let go of it, and just keep writing.

Takeoff and Departure

Scissors
cut paper

Paper
wraps
stone

THE
RULES

Stone
blunts
scissors

Part 135 Standard Instrument Takeoff Minimums

1 or 2 ENGINE AIRCRAFT	3 OR MORE ENGINES
1 SM Visibility	½ SM Visibility

(FAR 91.175)

On an *AeroNav* approach chart, (formerly *NACO*), the triangle T symbol indicates that non-standard takeoff minimums apply.

Jeppesen charts provide the Part 135 takeoff minimums on the airport diagram page.

IFR Takeoff, Part 91

It is true that you can legally depart in zero-zero conditions – but *legal* does not mean that such operations are **smart**!

*Don't depart unless the airport's weather is at or above **landing** minimums.*
If you must depart in weather that's below landing minimums, select a nearby "takeoff alternate" with VFR or alternate weather minimums. If you experience a problem, you'll have a viable place to land.

"Fly Runway Heading" *(Reference the Pilot/Controller Glossary)*

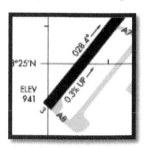

When cleared for takeoff, and directed to "fly runway heading," pilots are expected to maintain the heading that corresponds with the extended centerline of the departure runway. For example, referencing the KGYR Airport Diagram, Runway 03 has an actual magnetic heading of 028.4° – that's the runway heading and it's flown from liftoff. **Drift correction shall not be applied.**

ODPs (Obstacle Departure Procedures)

o Do not assume that "cleared as filed" or "cleared direct to" a fix means that you will be clear of terrain and/or obstacles without using the ODP.

o Regulations don't require the use of an ODP, and the *Controller Handbook* indicates that it's up to the pilot.

o You don't need a clearance to fly an ODP, but at a non-towered airport, ATC <u>assumes</u> that you'll use one.

o The pilot is responsible for terrain clearance until ATC issues a radar vector, or clears the aircraft off of the ODP.

o At unfamiliar airports, one should follow the ODP in IMC or at night.

o Airports that don't have an instrument approach, (and a few that do), <u>don't have an ODP</u>.

o Before you fly, study the charts and talk to other pilots.

Jeppesen prints ODPs at the bottom of the runway diagram page. *AeroNav, (*formerly *NACO)*, puts them in Section C of the approach charts in the "*Takeoff Minimums and Obstacle Departure Procedures"* section — The Triangle T pages.

▽ TAKE-OFF MINIMUMS AND (OBSTACLE) DEPARTURE PROCEDURES ▽

Never fly in the same cockpit with someone braver than you!!

ODP and Takeoff Minimums - Example

> **VERNAL, UT**
> VERNAL RGNL
> TAKE-OFF MINIMUMS: **Rwy 16**, 1500-2 or std with a min. climb
> of 250' per NM to 7000'. **Rwy 25**, 1500-2 or std. with a min. climb
> of 390' per NM to 7000. **Rwy 34**, 1600-2 or std. with a min. climb
> of 330' per MM to 7000'
> **DEPARTURE PROCEDURE:** Rwys 7, 34, turn right. Rwys 16,
> 25, turn left. All aircraft climb direct VEL. Aircraft departing V391
> S-bound climb on course. All others climb in holding patter (SE,
> right turns, 332o inbound). Aircraft SW-bound V208 depart VEL
> at or above 8400', all others depart VEL at or above 9500'.
> Continue climb on course to MEA or assigned altitude.

Some ODPs are graphically displayed like a SID, like the EXCON
ONE DEPARTURE (RNAV) (OBSTACLE) in Apple Valley, CA
(KAPV).

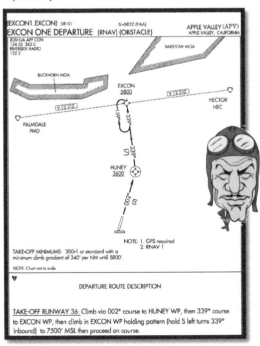

*If an ODP hasn't
been published for
the airport, the
following will be
indicated:*
*"TAKE-OFF
MINIMUMS: IFR
departure not
authorized."*
*This prevents Part
135 operators from
performing a takeoff
in IMC.*

Standard Instrument Departures (SIDs) or Departure Procedures (DPs)

- JEPPESEN SIDs are in front of each applicable airport's section. *AeroNav's* SID Index is in the *"INDEXES OF TERMINAL CHARTS AND MINIMUMS"* pages.
- A SID or DP will keep aircraft away from the terrain.
- To legally fly a SID, you'll need an ATC clearance and at a minimum, the SID or DP's <u>textual</u> description.
- To file a SID or DP, start the flight plan with the SID's code. For instance, Las Vegas' COWBY FOUR DEPARTURE code is: (COWBY4.COWBY). It ends, or transitions at COWBY.

(COWBY4.COWBY) 11013

COWBY FOUR DEPARTURE (RNAV)   SL-662 (FAA)   LAS VEGAS

- Some SIDs have multiple transitions. For instance, in addition to the SLI (Seal Beach) transition, shown below . . .

(ANAHM3.SLI) 09015

ANAHEIM THREE DEPARTURE   SANTA ANA/JOHN   SL-377 (FAA)

. . . the *ANAHEIM THREE DEPARTURE* has HEC, LHS and VTU transitions:

HECTOR TRANSITION (ANAHM3.HEC): From over SLI VORTAC via SLI R-058 and PDZ R-238 to PDZ VORTAC, then via PDZ R-012 and HEC R-232 to HEC VORTAC.

LAKE HUGHES TRANSITION (ANAHM3.LHS): From over SLI VORTAC via SLI R-058 and PDZ R-238 to POXKU INT, then via POM R-164 to BAYJY INT, then via VNY R-095 to DARTS INT. Thence via SLI R-319 and LHS R-139 to LHS VORTAC.

VENTURA TRANSITION (ANAHM3.VTU): From over SLI VORTAC via SLI R-251 to WILMA INT, then via LAX R-123 to LAX VORTAC, then via LAX R-276 and VTU R-093 to VTU VOR/DME.

RNAV (Area Navigation) SIDs

(BOACH4.BOACH) 11013

BOACH FOUR DEPARTURE (RNAV)

Requires a Flight Management System (FMS) or an IFR certified GPS.

Opting out of the SID

Enter *"No SID"* in the REMARKS section.

Climb Gradients

A specified minimum climb gradient could be required to fly a SID or ODP, especially if mountains are involved.
Below is the climb gradient required for the *Tucson 7 Departure:*

TAKE-OFF MINUMUMS

Rwys 3, 11L/R, 29L/R: Standard with minimum climb of 400' per NM to 9900.

Rwy 21: Standard with minimum climb of 380' per NM to 9900'.

AeroNav and *Jeppesen* both publish tables to convert a **feet per nm** gradient to a **rate of climb in feet per minute.**

If you can't locate the RATE OF CLIMB tables, do the math.

If you know your Ground Speed (GS):

$$\frac{\text{Climb Gradient} \times GS}{60} = \text{Ft/min}$$

For example, if taking off on Tucson's RWY 11L or 11R, the required climb gradient is 400 feet per nautical mile (nm).

TAKE-OFF MINUMUMS

Rwys 3, 11L/R, 29L/R: Standard with minimum climb of 400' per NM to 9900.

$\frac{400}{60} \times 100 = 666$ Using a 100 knot climb **ground speed**, this climb gradient requires 666 feet per minute rate of climb to 9,900 feet MSL.

"Standard" takeoff minimums apply to Part 135 operators, but Part 91 operators would be wise to also follow the required climb gradient.

Takeoff Weather and its affect on Climb Gradients

Some airports offer lower takeoff minimums if an aircraft can meet or exceed a specified climb gradient. For example:

HOME TOWN AIRPORT, WI
HOME TOWN MUNI
TAKE-OFF MINIMUMS: **Rwy 34**, 1500-2 or std. with a min. climb of 325 per NM to 4000.

Part 135 operators, flying one or two engine aircraft can takeoff on runway 34 with as low as 1 mile visibility (standard). The aircraft must, however, climb to 4,000' at **325'** per nautical mile to 4,000 feet MSL – **542 FPM** all the way to 4,000 feet.

.

IFR Altitudes

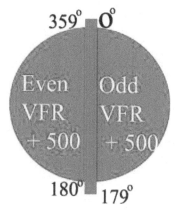

o *Controlled Airspace* –
ATC <u>can</u> clear you to fly at an EVEN or ODD altitude, regardless of your magnetic track heading.

o *Uncontrolled Airspace* –
you **must** fly the correct hemispheric altitude based on your track. (FAR 91.179)

VFR on Top (AIM 4-4-8)

This starts with an IFR flight plan and an IFR clearance. Once on top of the clouds and able to maintain VFR cloud clearance, you may declare "VFR on top." Here are the procedures you must now follow:

- o Fly the appropriate hemispheric VFR altitudes.
- o VFR cloud clearances and visibility now apply.
- o Follow VFR **and** IFR rules.
- o Report changes in altitude to ATC.
- o Separation from other traffic may not happen. The pilot is responsible for seeing and avoiding all aircraft.
- o Clearance to operate "VFR-on-top in VFR conditions" does not imply cancellation of the IFR flight plan, so don't forget to close your flight plan or cancel IFR.

Cruise Clearance (AIM 4-4-3)

- o ATC will assign a block of airspace – any altitude from the minimum IFR altitude up to and including the altitude specified in the clearance.
  - For example: "Bonanza 34 Delta Bravo, cleared to the Natchitoches Airport, cruise three thousand".
- o You can level off or climb or descend in this block of airspace. However, once the pilot reports that he or she is descending from an altitude in the block of airspace, he or she may not return/climb without additional ATC clearance.

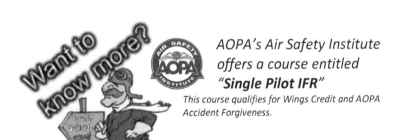

AOPA's Air Safety Institute offers a course entitled "Single Pilot IFR"

This course qualifies for Wings Credit and AOPA Accident Forgiveness.

Flashlights are tubular metal containers kept in a flight bag for the purpose of storing dead batteries!

When one engine fails on a twin-engine airplane you

always have enough power left to get you to the scene of the crash.

Cockpit NEXRAD Weather

When needed, NEXRAD Weather is invaluable. However, having it in your cockpit it doesn't make you invincible, and there are several limitations that you should understand.

Latency and Other Limitations

The **time stamp** on the display shown above, "W_x—00:06" means that it has been six minutes since the National Weather Service provided the information. However, the depicted weather could be older, since it takes a few minutes to upload the weather.
In this case, "W_x—00:06" <u>could mean</u> the weather is twelve minutes old!

AOPA's Air Safety Institute offers two online interactive courses, ***"IFR Insights: Cockpit Weather"*** *and* ***"Datalink".*** *Both courses qualify for AOPA Accident Forgiveness and the FAA Wings program.*

NEXRAD

(**NEX**t Generation **RAD**ar) finds precipitation, but it doesn't see clouds or turbulence. Strong returns, like the one shown here, infer turbulence.

Reflectivity
Weather Radar scans the sky at various degrees, taking pictures in 14 slices, like a medical CT scan.

Composite reflectivity shows the highest dBZ, (strongest reflected energy), at all of the elevation scans or slices, not just the reflected energy at a single elevation scan. XM Radio's NEXRAD images are composite images.

Base reflectivity shows reflected energy from scans at the lower elevations. Lower meaning, at and below 7,000 feet near the station, and as high as 14,000 feet 120 miles away.

The NEXRAD displays from **http://aviationweather.gov/** *default to "composite reflectivity", but you can choose to see a "base reflectivity"*

Weather and Radar Processor (WARP)

Center controllers use a weather radar system called WARP. It's based on NEXRAD radar data and it's quite good. However, it doesn't display light precipitation. There's also a delay or latency.

NEXRAD's Color Codes

Green – Light Precip.
Yellow/Orange – Moderate Precip.
Red – Strong Precip.
Purple – Extreme Precip.

Adding to the NEXRAD Picture

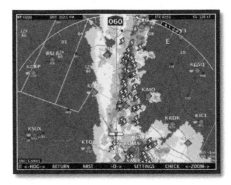

Lightning strikes are associated with convective activity, and help confirm the presence of a thunderstorm and turbulence.
However, the reverse isn't true – the absence of lightning strikes doesn't indicate the lack of convective activity.

Motion
Avoid storms cells that move 20 knots or faster. This would indicate the presence of strong convective activity.

Shared Energy
As cells move closer to one another, they begin to share energy and become higher, stronger and more turbulent.

Satellite Mosaic
Infrared Satellite Images
Warmer, low lying clouds are depicted in gray, while colder, high clouds are depicted in a whiter color. These whiter clouds indicate convection & turbulence.

Echo Tops come from **NEXRAD** and indicate the highest altitude at which precipitation is falling. Higher tops indicate convection & turbulence.

Contours – Tight contours, (the rapid change from green to yellow to red and or purple), indicate convection and turbulence.

Avoid:

- Heavy rain
- Lightning strikes
- Steep gradients
- Tops that are above 30,000 feet
- Cells that are moving faster than 15 mph
- Any precipitation associated with a convective cell. If a radar echo is depicted with a red center, treat the entire return as if it were red.
- Avoid cells by at least 20 miles. Severe turbulence can extend far from the edges of the return.

Common Sense Holding

Step 1 – Diagram ATC's instructions. For example, if you are instructed to:

"Hold on the Fairfield (FFU) 270 degree radial, 40 DME fix."

40 DME   FFU

Step 2 – Visualize your position on the chart or approach plate, and mark it. Then, chop the holding pattern in half, (as shown below).

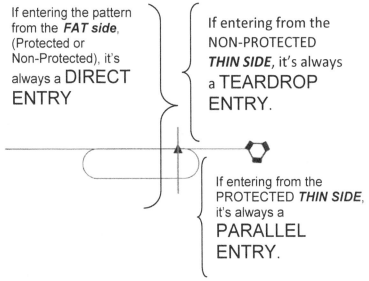

If entering the pattern from the **FAT side**, (Protected or Non-Protected), it's always a DIRECT ENTRY

If entering from the NON-PROTECTED **THIN SIDE**, it's always a TEARDROP ENTRY.

If entering from the PROTECTED **THIN SIDE**, it's always a PARALLEL ENTRY.

Basic Holding Rules
- o   STANDARD PATTERNS – RIGHT turns
- o   NON-STANDARD PATTERNS – LEFT turns

Holding times:

- **At or below** 14,000' MSL – Hold 1 Min.
- **Above** 14,000' MSL — Hold 1 1/2 Min.
  - The outbound timing starts when wings level or abeam the fix, whichever occurs **last**.

Holding Airspeeds

At least three minutes before the estimated arrival at the holding fix, slow to holding airspeed:

Up to 6,000' MSL, hold at:	200 KIAS maximum
6,000' to 14,000' MSL, hold at:	230 KIAS maximum
Above 14,000' MSL, hold at:	265 KIAS maximum
Unless depicted otherwise	

Correcting the Inbound Time (1 Min. Pattern example)

- If the trip *inbound* to the fix is less than 1 minute, adjust the outbound leg by 2/3 the difference. For instance, if the inbound trip takes 40 seconds. 2/3 of the 20 second difference is 14 seconds. Fly the next outbound leg for 74 seconds.
- If the *inbound* trip exceeds 1 minute, adjust the outbound time by 1/3 the difference. For instance, if the inbound leg took 80 seconds. 1/3 of the 20 second difference is 7 seconds. Fly the next outbound leg for 53 seconds.

> **LESS than the 1 or 1 ½ minutes** — adjust by **MORE** (2/3).
> **MORE than the 1 or 1 ½ minutes** — adjust by **LESS** (1/3).

Correcting Course

The HDG correction needed to maintain the inbound course should be doubled on the outbound leg. For instance, if you have a 5° crab on the inbound leg, apply a 10° correction on the outbound leg.

The Pop UP Clearance

Converting from VFR to an IFR Clearance

Contact the ATC facility that controls your current airspace. For example, "Kansas City Center, Cessna 456 Charlie Alpha, VFR 30 miles Northwest of Hutchinson, request". Just start with those words because unless you're already with a controller (VFR flight following), your first attempt may not hit the right frequency.

Once you have the right controller, you can be more specific: "Kansas City Center, Cessna 456 Charlie Alpha, we are going to need an **IFR clearance** for the rest of our flight to Wichita." Including the words "IFR clearance" removes any chance of misunderstanding. The controller knows that you want a real IFR clearance, not just a vector or flight following.

Controllers handle "Pop-Up" IFR clearances on a workload basis. If the controller is too busy for your IFR conversion, you'll need to contact Flight Service, and using the standard flight plan format, file an IFR flight plan to your destination.

Start your flight plan at a NAVAID or intersection that's ideally 20 miles prior to the weather ahead. This should give you time to file and let your clearance move through the system – from Flight Service to the controller who will grant your clearance. Remember to check the charts to ensure that you're at or above the MEA for the route.

As you approach the starting NAVAID or fix, call ATC and ask for your IFR clearance. They can't turn you down.

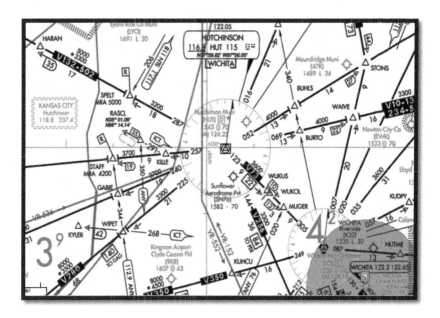

It's best to start your flight plan on an airway, but if you can't find a good airway, fix or NAVAID, you can name a point, such as "the Hutchinson VORTAC 270 radial at 30 DME."

You don't need to end your flight plan at an airport. It could end at a VMC NAVAID or fix – somewhere that's clear of clouds, so you descend for landing.

Filing a STAR

AeroNav's presentation of Houston's GLAND THREE ARRIVAL (KIAH), (GLAND.GLAND3), requires two pages, with the ARRIVAL DESCRIPTION on page 2.

If you plan to join the STAR at Corpus Christi (CRP), file: CRP.GLAND3.

- o Some transitions are "**ATC assigned**", like the KAWSE-1, KAWSE-3 & MILNY transitions, shown below. You should not file those transitions.
- o **As a minimum,** you must have the STAR's textual description in the cockpit.

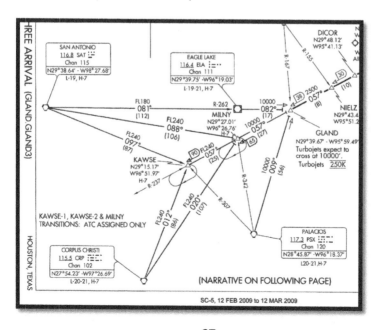

Opting Out of a STAR

Enter *"No STAR"* in the remarks section of the flight plan.

RNAV STARS require FMS or GPS

RNAV STARS have published mandatory speeds and / or crossing altitudes. Published expected altitudes and speeds are for **planning purposes only**.

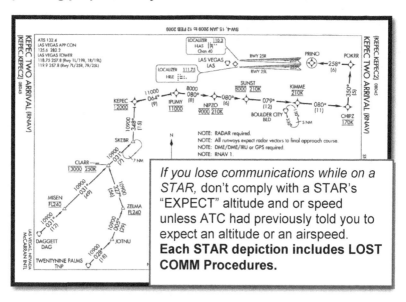

If you lose communications while on a STAR, don't comply with a STAR's "EXPECT" altitude and or speed unless ATC had previously told you to expect an altitude or an airspeed. **Each STAR depiction includes LOST COMM Procedures.**

Possible RNAV STAR Clearances

o "Cleared HADLY ONE arrival, descend and maintain 12,000."
  - **Translation:** You are cleared to navigate laterally, and descent to 12,000 feet.
o "Cleared HADLY ONE arrival."
  - **Translation:** You may navigate laterally ONLY.
o "Descend via the HADLY ONE arrival."
  - **Translation:** Those are the magic words! You may now navigate laterally and vertically; descending via the STAR's altitude restrictions.

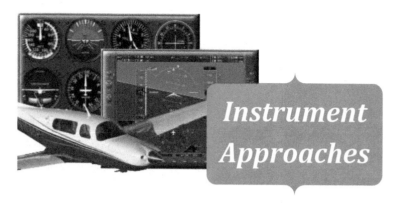

Instrument Approaches

Briefing the Approach

Do it out loud! There's something about verbalizing the approach that etches the information in the memory.

After obtaining the current weather, start your briefing with the information in the top briefing box:

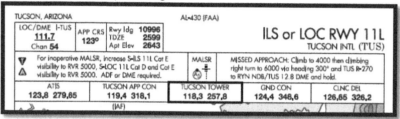

Things to consider while briefing:

- o That the proper and current approach plate is selected. (Approaches are effective 0901Z on the day specified).
- o That the correct NAVAIDs are tuned and identified.
- o That the marker audio is ON.
- o If it's a RNAV/GPS approach, ensure that the correct approach has been selected on the GPS.
- o Commit to memory the Missed Approach procedure's first heading and altitude.
- o What type of runway and approach lighting can you expect?
- o Is the lighting Pilot Controlled?

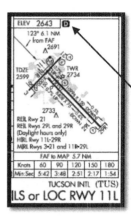

Check the runway diagram for:

- o Runway lighting types, such as HIRL, MIRL, etc.
- o Approach lighting
- o REIL
- o PAPI, VASI & PLASI

The negative "D" indicates that runway declared distance information is available in the A/FD, where the distance information is broken down into:

- o TORA: Take off run available,
- o TODA: Take off distance available,
- o ASDA: Accelerate stop distance, available &
- o LDA: Landing distance available

Two Types of Pilot Controlled Lighting (PCL)

- o Single Intensity, non adjustable PCL. The pilot keys the microphone three or five times (as specified), within five seconds.
- o HIRL or MIRL PCL. The pilot keys the microphone within five seconds:
  - 3 times – HIRL or MIRL – for lowest intensity; (Lower the REIL intensity or turn REIL off)
  - 5 times – HIRL or MIRL – for medium or lower intensity; (Lower REIL intensity or REIL off)
  - 7 times – HIRL – for highest intensity; (REIL on).

When either type of system is activated, a 15-minute countdown starts, after which the lights turn off unless someone makes the appropriate amount of clicks on the appropriate frequency.

70

Next, look at the profile view

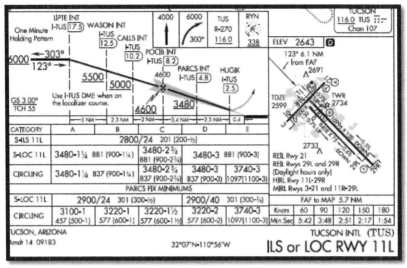

Things to consider while briefing:

- o **Precision Approach:**
  - The step down altitude(s), the glide slope interception altitude, the altitude at which you'll cross the marker, and the approximate rate of descent in Feet per Minute.
  - The DH and the weather required.
  - As a backup to the ILS, what is the Localizer MDA?

- o **Non-precision approach:**
  - Step down altitude(s).
  - If a VDP is not indicated, calculate a VDP for a 3^0 glide slope, and the approximate rate of descent in Feet per Minute.
  - The MDA and the weather required.
  - The runway's length, lighting, VASI/PAPI, etc.
  - FAF to the MAP – the distance and time.

Look at the "bird's eye" view

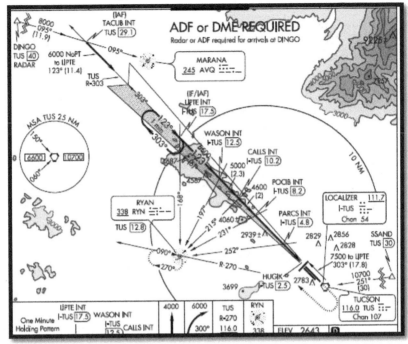

Read the notes, and consider:

- o MSA, highest obstruction(s) and terrain.
- o Notes and warnings.
- o Important NAVAIDs and courses.

Finally, look at the airport diagram and consider:

- o The planned runway exit and potential hot spots
- o Your taxi plan – from the runway to the ramp.

Don't forget the GPS

If you have a GPS, don't forget to "brief" it too. Scroll through the approach and the missed approach waypoints and make sure everything is there.

Approach Clearance

If a feeder route to an IAF begins at a fix located along the route of flight that precedes the holding fix, and clearance for an approach is issued, you should commence the approach via the published feeder route.

A Blank Check

Sometimes ATC may not specify a particular approach procedure in the clearance, but may say, **"Cleared Approach."** That means you can execute any of the authorized approaches for that airport. This clearance **does not** authorize a Contact or Visual approach.

Using the Autopilot, Part 135 Operations (FAR 135.95)

o   It may be engaged in the descent through no lower than 500' AGL, except when flying an instrument approach.
  * When flying a non-precision approach, disengage at no lower than 50 feet above the MDA.
  * When flying an ILS approach, the autopilot must be disengaged no lower than 50 feet above the terrain.

 Memory Helpers for the Approach

A-B-C M-A-I-D

A	ATIS
B	Brief the approach.
C	Checklist.
M	Marker Beacon Audio ON.
A	Altimeter SET (Also, set the bug to the MDA/DH).
I	Indicators (Set frequencies, courses, etc.).
D	DG SET, unless you are fortunate enough to have an HSI.

Approach Basics, applying to all approaches

- o Brief the approach and accomplish **ABC MAID**.
- o You may descend from ATC's assigned altitude to the published altitude that begins the approach when you are "**10-10 and Cleared**." (Within 10 nm of the runway, 10⁰ of the approach course, and cleared for the approach).
  - ATC won't turn you over to the tower controller unless you are established on the final approach course.

Procedure Turns

At the initial approach fix, slow to approach speed. Depending on the wind, fly outbound for 2 to 4 minutes. Remain within 10 nm, or as charted on the approach.

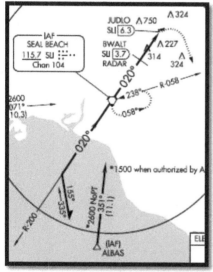

THEN . . .
Turn 45°, as charted and fly for 1 to 2 minutes.
This is a good time to check that the heading indicator matches the magnetic compass.

THEN . . .
Start a 180° turn, as charted, to intercept the inbound course.

Report "Procedure turn inbound", or as directed by ATC.

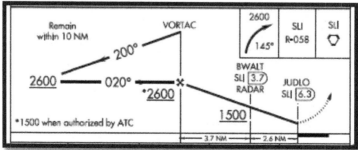

Holding Pattern in Lieu of a Procedure Turn

- o Hold as depicted.
- o Don't exceed the protected or designated holding airspace.
- o Descend in the holding pattern.
- o Report "Procedure turn inbound", or as directed by ATC

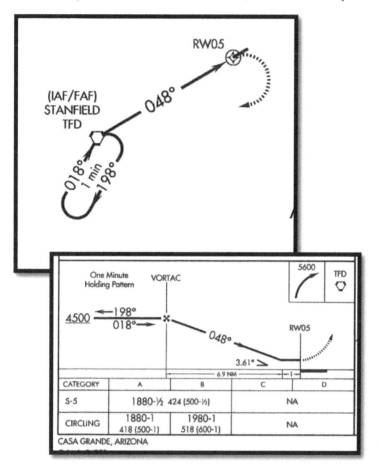

Arcing and Leading the Arc

It takes 2 minutes to make a standard rate, 360° turn. Therefore, to turn 90°, a standard rate turn requires 30 seconds.

- o   Determine your ground speed and convert it to nautical miles per minute, by dividing the GS by 60.
- o   Because you'll need 30 seconds to make the 90° turn, divide the **miles per minute** by two – giving you the number of nautical miles that you'll need to "lead the turn":

If your GS is:	Divide miles per minute by 2:	Lead the turn by:
100 knots / 60 = **1.7** miles/min	**1.7** / 2 =	**.85** (8/10) nm
120 knots / 60 = **2** miles/min	**2** / 2 =	**1** nm
150 knots / 60 = **2.5** miles/min	**2.5** / 2 =	**1.25** nm (1 ¼) nm

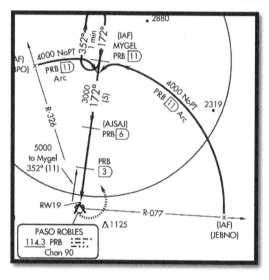

Arcing:

Situation: Flying westward toward JEBNO, established on PRB's 077° radial.

If your ground speed is 120 knots, one mile before JEBNO and the arc, turn RIGHT 90°, to 347°.

Roll out on heading 347°, and select the next 10° bearing TO the station — **247°**.

(The CDI/HSI needle should be off to the left).

As the CDI/HSI moves from the left to the center, select the next 10° bearing change, (**237°**). Turn left as necessary to stay on the 11 DME arc.

Arcing Travel Tips

- ○ *If you're inside the arc, don't make any turns toward the VOR until you again catch the desired arc.*
- ○ *If you are outside the arc, make a 20° correction to return to the arc.*
- ○ **For clockwise arcing**: *the next radial inbound course will be +10°. Turn your OBS* **clockwise** *as you arc.*
- ○ **For counter clockwise arcing**: *the next radial inbound course will be minus 10°. Turn your OBS* **counter clockwise** *as you arc.*

Intercepting a Radial from the Arc

Miles from the VOR	Degrees per nautical mile
10 miles	6°
15 miles	4°
30 miles	2°
60 miles	1°

- ○ At 120 knots, a 90° turn takes 1 nm. If you're on the 10 nm arc, a 90° turn takes 1 nm or 6 degrees to lead the radial.
- ○ At 100 knots, on the 10 nm arc, a 90° turn takes .85 nm. .85 x 6° = 5.1° to lead the radial.
- ○ At 150 knots, on the 10 nm arc, a 90° turn takes 1.25 nm. 1.25 x 6° = 7.5° to lead the radial.

ILS Approach

- ○ Assuming that the LOC approach is your backup approach, start the timer at the FAF.
- ○ You may descend from the ATC assigned altitude to the published altitude that begins the approach when you are "**10-10 and Cleared.**" (Within 10 nm of the runway, 10° of the approach course, and cleared for the approach).

To avoid false glide slopes, (9° and 15° descent angles), you must intercept the GS from below.

Note your altitude as you pass "the marker" and compare that altitude to the charted altitude shown in the profile view. For example, on the TUS ILS 11L, you should cross *POCIB* intersection at 4,600 feet.

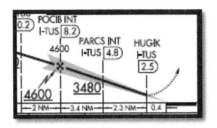

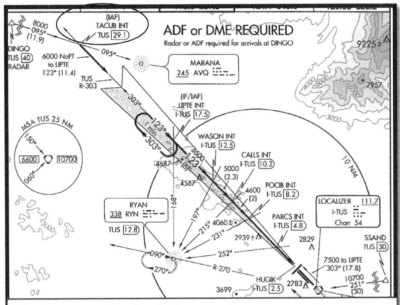

If being vectored for the final approach course, never leave ATC's previously assigned altitude until you are on a published segment of the approach. Reference the KTUS *ILS or LOC RWY 11L* approach, shown here, the *published segment* is denoted by **heavy black lines,** starting at **TACUB** intersection, and the segment altitude is 6,000 feet.

To quickly calculate the target descent rate for an ILS's 3° glide slope:
Ground speed X 5 = Feet per minute rate of descent.
EXAMPLE: 100 knots GS X 5 = 500 FPM target descent rate.

VASI and the ILS Approach (FAR 91.129)

If a runway has an operational VASI, you must remain at or above the glide slope until a lower altitude is necessary for landing.

ILS/LOC & VOR Approaches

- Monitor the ILS/LOC or VOR receiver's Morse code.
- Use both receivers for a VOR approach.

LOC and BC Approach

- The Back Course approach must be a published approach, (Not a homemade approach)
- Always set the Front Course in the CDI or HSI. If you have an HSI, it might have a reverse sensing capability.
- If you don't have reverse sensing capability, then you must "steer away" from the localizer needle when flying inbound on the LOC BC.

- Start timing at the FAF.

Contact Approach (AIM 5-4-23)

- It's never assigned by ATC – You must request it.
- ATC will provide separation between IFR and Special VFR traffic.
- The airport must have an instrument approach procedure and 1 mile visibility.

In addition, you should:
- Stay clear of clouds &
- Firmly believe that you'll continue to the airport successfully.

No Gyro Approach

- When ATC says "Turn left" or "Turn Right", start the turn immediately.
- When you hear, "Stop turn", stop the turn immediately.
- ATC will instruct you to make half standard rate turns on final.

Sidestep Approaches

As soon as the runway to which you're cleared to land is in sight, begin a sidestep maneuver to the extended centerline of the landing runway.

Circling Approach

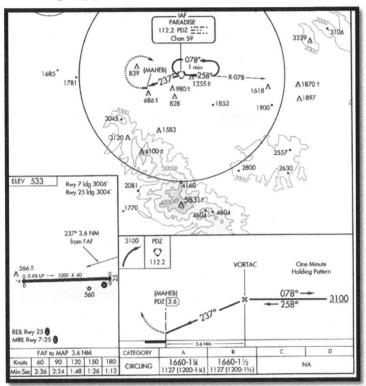

If the final approach exceeds the runway alignment factor of 30°, or 15° in the case of a GPS approach, this mandates the design of a circling approach. *(AIM 5-4-20)*

The VOR or GPS-A to Corona (KAJO), shown above, has a final approach course of 237° to Runway 25. That's only about 15° off, and yet it's a circling approach. **WHY?** Look at the profile view. A straight-in approach would require a descent from 3,100' MSL to the 533' MDA in 3.6 nm. If you never leveled off at the MDA, and dove for the end of the runway, you'd need to lose 2,567' and you'd need to lose it *FAST* . . . at over 700 feet per mile! That's a 7° glide path . . . . way too steep for a straight in approach.

81

Circling Travel Tips

- *The circling radius for a category A aircraft is 1.3 nm, so don't wander too far from the runway, and never turn your back to the runway.*
- *If you find yourself in IMC conditions after initiating a circling maneuver in VMC, execute a Missed Approach.**
- *Fly the circling approach as close to pattern altitude as possible. Circling minimums only provide 300 feet of obstacle clearance.*

*Circling Missed Approach

Start a climb toward the landing runway, and then follow the Missed Approach Procedure.

Descending below the MDA/DH/DA (FAR 91.175)
You cannot descend below the MDA/DH/DA unless:

- You're in a position to land on the intended runway using a normal rate of descent and normal maneuvers. (Part 121 & 135 operators must land in the touchdown zone).
- You determine that flight visibility is at or above that which is required to complete the approach.

If the approach lights are in sight, you may descend to **100 feet above the Touchdown Zone Elevation (TDZE).** *You may descend lower than 100 feet above the TDZE, if either of these are clearly visible:*

- The Red Terminating Bars (ALSF 1 system)
- The Red Side Row Bars (ALSF 2 system)

In the absence of an approach lighting system, you may descend below the MDA/DH/DA and land if any of the following are in sight:

- REIL,
- VASI,
- Runway, runway markings, or runway lights,
- Touchdown zone, touchdown markings or touchdown lights,
- Threshold, threshold markings or threshold lights.

Approach, Part 91 Operations

If the weather conditions are reported to be below minimums, you can still try the approach, just to "take a look". However, you must never descend below minimums, unless *FAR 91.175* criteria are met. (See the previous page)

Approach Lighting Systems

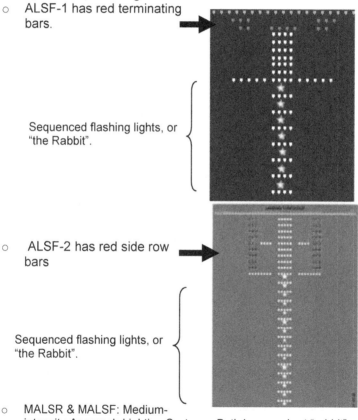

- ○ **ALSF-1 and ALSF-2:** Both have Sequenced Flashing Lights, commonly known as "the rabbit". Both systems are 2,400' to 3,000' long.
- ○ ALSF-1 has red terminating bars.

    Sequenced flashing lights, or "the Rabbit".

- ○ ALSF-2 has red side row bars

    Sequenced flashing lights, or "the Rabbit".

- ○ MALSR & MALSF: Medium-intensity Approach Lighting Systems. Both have a short "rabbit" and are 1,400' long (1/4 mile+)
- ○ SALS: Simple Approach Lighting System.
- ○ SSALS: Simplified Short Approach Lighting System.
- ○ SSALR & SSALF: Simplified Short Approach Lighting System with a short "rabbit". 1,400' long (1/4 mile+)

Visual Descent Point (VDP)

The Missed Approach Point or MAP is never located where a pilot could start a nice 3° descent for landing. It's more likely to be located at the runway threshold.

That's why the FAA came up with the **Visual Descent Point**, or **VDP**. This lets you decide if you want to initiate a missed approach, before you reach the MAP. The VDP allows a 3° descent angle, (300 feet per mile), to the landing zone.

If you can see the runway at the VDP, you may start a descent to the runway.

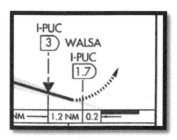

Reference the ILS/LOC DME, RWY 36 at KPUC:

The LOC's VDP has been established at I-PUC's 3 DME, which is **1.4** miles from the end of the runway.

At 1.4 miles, and at the LOC approach's MDA – 6240, that's **377'** above the runway threshold altitude.

S-LOC 36	6240-1 377 (300-1)

$\frac{377}{1.4}$ = 2.69° angle of descent or 269 feet per mile

If you delayed your descent 2/10 of a mile past the VDP, you would be 1.2 miles from the runway end, still allowing for a very comfortable **3.14°** descent angle or **314** feet per mile.

$\frac{377}{1.2}$ = 3.14° angle of descent or 314 feet per mile

To convert a 3° glide slope descent into feet per minute, glance at the GPS's ground speed and multiply that number by 5. For example:

120 knots ground speed x **5 = 600** feet per minute.

No Published VDP

If you have DME or a GPS, you can figure your own VDP.
Divide the approach procedure's height above touchdown (HAT) by
a descent gradient of 3^0 (300 feet per nautical mile).

Example for a HAT of 653 feet:

$$\frac{653}{300} = 2.17 \text{ VDP}$$

If we are what we eat, then some
pilots should eat more chicken.

Visual Descent Angles (VDAs)

VDAs appear on some non-precision approaches <u>for information purposes only</u>. VDAs establish a stabilized descent from the FAF or step-down fix, meeting the VDP at the MDA, where the pilot, (if the runway environment is spotted), can safely land.

Reference the Oxnard (KOXR) VOR RWY 25 approach, the **V**isual **D**escent **A**ngle (VDA), depicted between the FAF and the MAP, is **3.37°**.

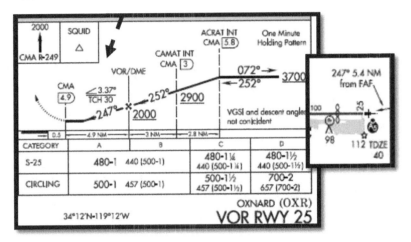

Drop the decimal point from the VDA to convert the 3.37° angle of descent to **337 feet per nautical mile.**

 o Convert the Ground Speed into miles per minute. If the anticipated GS is 120, that's the same as 2 miles per minute. (**120/60 = 2**).

 o Multiply miles per minute by the number of feet per nautical mile required in the descent.

2 x 337 = a descent rate of **674** feet per minute.

ILS Frequency Sharing

Some airports have an ILS approach to both ends of the runway. Detroit's Metro Airport (KDTW) has ILS approaches to both 4R and 22L. Both ILS frequencies are the same, (110.7), but the ILS identifications are different – I-DTW for 4R, and I-DWC for 22L. The different IDs mean each runway has its own LOC & GS transmitter.

Missed Approaches

After you have intercepted the approach's final approach course, set the Heading BUG, (if you have one), on the missed approach heading. Set the missed approach altitude in the altitude reminder, (if you have one), or write it down.

- o **PRECISION APPROACH:** Execute Missed Approach when you reach the Decision Altitude (DA).
- o **NON-PRECISION APPROACH:** Execute Missed Approach at the Missed Approach Point (MAP).
- o If "missing" from a circling approach, climb towards the landing runway, then execute the published procedure.
- o If you've made the decision to "go missed" before reaching the MAP, climb to the missed approach altitude, but continue the approach laterally to the MAP. Then, follow the published Missed Approach procedure.

When announcing to ATC that you're executing the "missed approach", include your intentions.

If you are practicing multiple instrument approaches, the tower or approach control may assign "**CLIMB OUT"** instructions that are contrary to the published missed approach procedure. In this case, when you initiate a "missed", the radio call is "**Climb out**", not "Missed approach."

Missed Approach Travel Tips

Don't try to memorize the entire missed approach procedure. Just remember the initial course or heading.

All Missed Approach Procedures begin with a climb, so initially:

- o *Power UP,*
- o *Nose UP,*
- o *Clean UP, &*
- o *Start the turn, if applicable*

Once safely in the climb, you can take a closer look at the procedure.

Unsuccessful Approach

If you have enough fuel to try another approach, and legally fly to your alternate, and you think you'll have a better chance on the next approach, then go for it. Proceed to your alternate, at or before you're short on fuel and ideas.

See Minimum/Emergency Fuel in the "When Things Go Wrong" section.

Experience is the knowledge that enables you to recognize a mistake when you make it again.

The Great Headwind/Tailwind Fable!
"WE'LL MAKE GOOD TIME ON THE WAY HOME!"

OH REALLY?

You're planning a cross country flight from Phoenix, AZ (KPHX) to Orange County, CA (KSNA) and back to KPHX – 300 nm each way.

- o Planned TAS is 100 knots.
- o The winds at altitude are 270 @ 50 knots, so you'll have a 50 knot head wind flying west to SNA, and, if the winds stay the same, a 50 knot tail wind, when you return to PHX.

Will your cumulative trip time be the same as if you had calm winds all day? Do you think that you'll make up for it on the return leg?

If you had calm winds, it would take:
KPHX-KSNA, (300 nm) @ 100 knots GS = 3 hours
KSNA-KPHX, (300 nm) @ 100 knots GS = 3 hours

Total trip time - 6 hours

If you had 50 knot headwinds flying west, and 50 knot tailwinds flying east, flight time would be:
KPHX-KSNA, (300 nm) @ 50 knots GS = 6 hours
KSNA-PHX, (300 nm) @ 150 knots GS = 2 hours

Total trip time - 8 hours

AOPA's Air Safety Institute offers several courses entitled "IFR Insights: Charts", "IFR Chart Challenge: VOR Approach", and "IFR Chart Challenge: ILS Approach"
These courses qualify for Wings Credit and AOPA Accident Forgiveness.

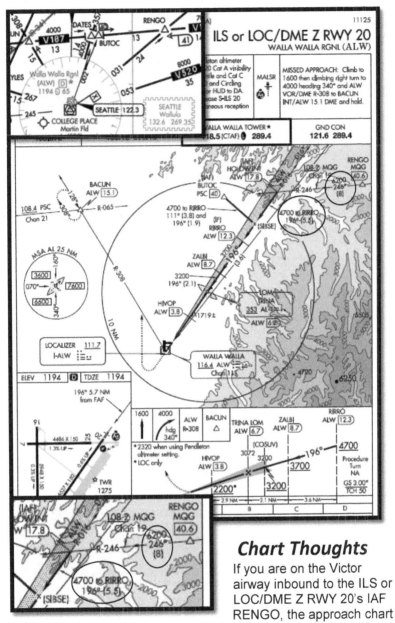

ILS or LOC/DME Z RWY 20
WALLA WALLA RGNL (ALW)

11125

Chart Thoughts

If you are on the Victor airway inbound to the ILS or LOC/DME Z RWY 20's IAF RENGO, the approach chart indicates that it's an 8 mile trip to the localizer (joining at the IAF HALOW), then another 5.5 to the Initial Fix - RIRRO.

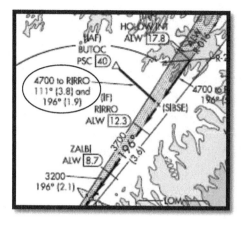

If you fly from BUTOC (IAF), to the localizer, the approach chart indicates two distances. The first distance, 3.8, is the distance to the localizer, joining at SIBSE. The second, 1.9, is the distance from the localizer and SIBSE to the IF - RIRRO

Using another approach, (ILS or LOC Y RWY 20), the approach chart indicates one distance from DATES: 8.5 from DATES to TRINA (LOM/IAF).

Conclusion

If two distances are given, the first is the distance to the inbound course/LOC interception. The second distance is from the course interception to the FAF/LOM or the IF.

Jim Terpstra, Senior Corporate Vice President of Flight Information Technology, retired, has written a series of articles that have been saved in AOPA Pilot Magazine's online archives. These help explain Jeppesen Airway Manual Navigational Charts.

http://www.jeppesen.com/personal -solutions/aviation/chart-clinic.jsp **Click on "Chart Clinic Reprints"**

From a safety standpoint, in our view one of the things that we do in the basic design is the pilot always has the ultimate authority of control. There's no computer on the airplane that he cannot override or turn off if the ultimate comes. In terms of any of our features, we don't inhibit that totally. We make it difficult, but if something in the box should behave inappropriately, the pilot can say 'This is wrong' and he can override it. That's a fundamental difference in philosophy that we have versus some of the competition. — John Cashman, Chief Test Pilot Boeing 777

Before You Fly Travel Tip
Check Jeppesen's GPS NavData® Alerts and
Database Cycles at: **http://Jeppesen.com**

GPS Approaches

You may fly an approach with your panel mounted
certified GPS, but only if the approach
indicates "**RNAV (GPS)**" or is an *"overlay"* on
an existing approach, such as a "**VOR or GPS**"
approach. It must have *GPS* in the title.

VOR or GPS-A
DY BRISCOE FIELD (MLF)

When selecting an overlay approach, the 430/530 approach menu
displays "GPS" in the title, for example, **VOR 03** ^{G}**Ps** .
NDB, VOR and TACAN approaches can be found in your database,
but unless the approach has "GPS" in the title, you cannot use the
approach. These non-GPS approaches are included in the
database for map reference only.

GPS Approach Rules

- ○ If you're flying an overlay approach, like a "VOR or GPS-A",
  or "NDB or GPS Rwy 24", back up the approach with your
  VOR or NDB, if installed.
- ○ In most cases, a GPS can substitute for ADF or DME.
  There is an exception:
  - • **ADF Approaches** – If
    the approach is not a
    GPS *overlay*, the
    aircraft must be
    equipped with an ADF.

NDB RWY 4R
CHANDLER MUNI (CHD)

- When cleared for a GPS approach, you must navigate to all the fixes.

Execute a missed approach:

- If a RAIM warning appears.
- If you have a Garmin 530/430, and within 2 nm of the final approach fix, it doesn't switch from **TERM** to **APR** or 0.3^nm
- If you have a Garmin 530W/430W, and within 2 nm of the final approach fix, it doesn't switch from **TERM** to either **LNAV, LPV, L/VNAV, or LNAV+V**

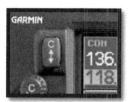

More Travel Tips

Holding down the Garmin 430 or 530 COM flip-flop key for about 3 seconds switches the active frequency to 121.5.

If you would like "DME" from an ILS localizer, you could enter the localizer identifier as a GPS waypoint. For example, I-HJT is entered as IHJT. (All localizer IDs are NOT in the database).

LOCALIZER 111.95
I-HJT ·-···
Chan 56 (Y)

GPS Waypoints in SIDs, STARs and Approaches

Fly-By Waypoint   Fly-Over Waypoint

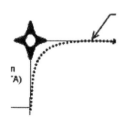   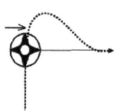   If the fix is circled, it's a FLY-OVER fix and you must fly over the fix <u>before</u> turning to the new course.

GPS and Database Limitations

o GPS systems are so good that we often forget that paper or electronic flight bag en-route charts, as well as departure, arrival and approach charts are still required and necessary for flight. Pilots need to verify – between the GPS and the paper chart or electronic flight bag chart – that all the waypoints or NAVAIDs are in the correct location.

o Not all instrument flight procedures can be coded into a SID, STAR, or approach procedure. "Uncodeable" procedures, like those containing radar vectors or complicated contingent instructions are not included in the database.

o Step-down fixes between the FAF/IF and MAP are not included in the database because not all systems can handle their inclusion. Your database may not include every leg or segment of a procedure.

o If you can't refer to an approach chart, you are not authorized to fly it.

o You should not fly approaches to private airports, or use helicopter approaches if you're not in a helicopter.

When passing each RNAV waypoint, think –
SOURCE, FORCE, and COURSE

o **SOURCE** — Verify that the correct SOURCE is being used for navigation, such as GPS or VLOC.

O **FORCE** — Verify that the correct GPS Mode is displayed:
  - Enroute ("ENR"),
  - Terminal ("TERM"), or
  - The final approach sensitivity annunciation:
    - **430/530 –**
      - "APR", or
      - "0.3^n_m" (ILS/LOC approaches)
    - **430W/530W –**
      - "LNAV",
      - "LPV",
      - "L/VNAV", or
      - "LNAV+V"

o **COURSE** — Put the proper *course* in the CDI/HSI. Don't wait to be prompted by the GPS.

Watching the WAAS and Non-WAAS

Watching the 430W/530W can be fascinating. However, you are still responsible for ensuring that holding patterns do not exceed the required time or distance, and that a procedure turn or holding in lieu of a procedure turn does not exceed the charted distance or time.

Enroute & Terminal Modes

Within 30 nm of the destination, the GNS 430 / 530 will switch from the **ENR**OUTE mode to the **TERM**INAL mode.
This results in a gradual GPS CDI scale transition from 5.0 nm to 1.0 nm – for a full scale deflection.

Approach: CDI Scale Transitions

GPS Approach, 430W/530W: If the FAF is the TO waypoint, and you are within 45° of the final approach course, the "TERM" annunciation changes to "LNAV", "LPV", "L/VNAV", or "LNAV+V".

GPS Approach, 430/530 non-WAAS: When within 2 nm of the FAF, the "TERM" annunciation changes to "APR".

VOR, LOC/ILS (ground signals)
As you approach the FAF:
The "TERM" annunciation in the lower left corner of the screen will change to:

- 430W/530W: "LNAV".
- 430/530 non-WAAS: "0.3^n_m".

Both "LNAV" and "0.3^n_m" mean that the <u>GPS CDI</u> scale is transitioning from 1.0 nm to 0.3 nm full scale deflection. You can also see it depicted on the Default NAV screen, (next page).

ILS Approach: The scale transition does not affect the CDI or HSI. It applies only to the CDI on the default NAV Page. The aircraft's CDI/HSI is coupled to the VOR or LOC receiver.

ILS Approaches

Reference the ILS 21 at Prescott, AZ (KPRC).

Prior to crossing the IAF – HUMTY, ensure that the Localizer frequency, 108.5, is in the active spot.

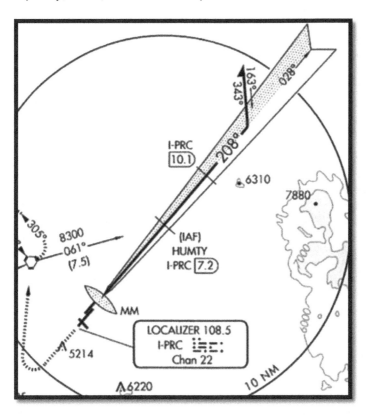

ILS Approaches and Auto Switching

If the LOC/ILS frequency is in the active spot, CDI/HSI coupling will automatically switch from the GPS receiver to the VLOC receiver as you complete the procedure turn inbound.

If you fail to switch the ILS frequency to the active frequency spot, a *"SELECT APPROPRIATE FREQUENCY FOR APPROACH"* message will appear within 3.0 nm of the FAF (Garmin **430/530**), or 2.0 nm of the FAF (Garmin **430W/530W**).

If within 2.0 nm of the FAF, and auto switching has not occurred, you must manually press the *CDI* key.

*The Automatic Switching feature works for ILS, SDF and LDA approaches, but **not for** LOC Backcourses.*

Vectors to Final

If you select an approach and choose the *"VECTORS TO FINAL" option*, this generates an extended line from the runway. The only "fixes" depicted are the runway and the final approach.

Vectors to Final Travel Tips

If you do choose the GPS's "Vectors to Final" option, you can bet that ATC will clear you to a fix outside the FAF, and you'll be all over the place trying to correct it.

*Select a full procedure, and if the procedure includes holding or a procedure turn, you can clear (**CLR**) those from the Flight Plan page.*

Z, Y, X, etc.

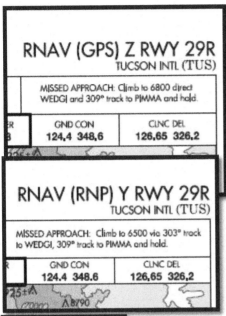

RNAV (GPS) Z RWY 29R
TUCSON INTL (TUS)

MISSED APPROACH: Climb to 6800 direct WEDGI and 309° track to PIMMA and hold.

	GND CON	CLNC DEL
R	**124.4 348.6**	**126.65 326.2**

RNAV (RNP) Y RWY 29R
TUCSON INTL (TUS)

MISSED APPROACH: Climb to 6500 via 303° track to WEDGI, 309° track to PIMMA and hold.

	GND CON	CLNC DEL
R	**124.4 348.6**	**126.65 326.2**

When multiple RNAV (GPS) approaches are published for the same runway, each approach is assigned a suffix from the <u>end</u> of the alphabet. The approach with the lowest minimums receives the Z suffix, the next lowest gets Y, and so forth.

RNP (*Required Navigation Performance*)

RNAV (GPS) and RNP systems are fundamentally similar, but RNP approaches sometimes have curved legs and require on-board performance monitoring and alerting. Crews flying RNP approaches require specialized training.

Don't drop the aircraft in order to fly the microphone.

WAAS and Non-WAAS GPS Minimums

LPV – Localizer Performance with Vertical Guidance

- o Requires a WAAS GPS.
- o LPV has a glide path.
- o Use **"LPV DA"** approach minimums.

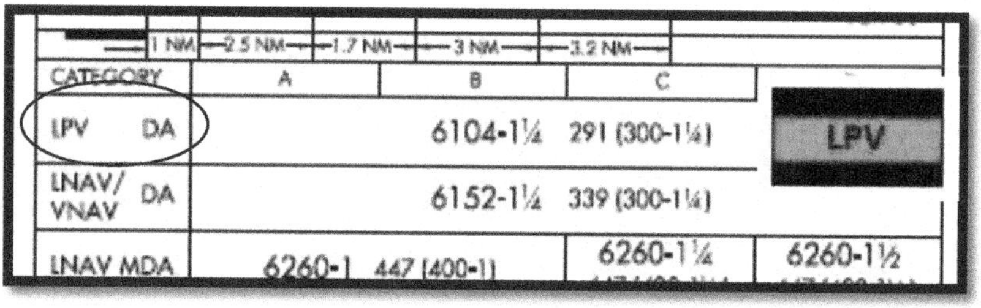

	1 NM	2.5 NM	1.7 NM	3 NM	3.2 NM	
CATEGORY		A		B	C	
LPV DA				6104-1¼ 291 (300-1¼)		LPV
LNAV/ DA VNAV				6152-1¼ 339 (300-1¼)		
LNAV MDA	6260-1 447 (400-1)			6260-1¼	6260-1½	

LNAV/VNAV – Lateral NAVigation and Vertical NAVigation

- o LNAV/VNAV approaches were developed to accommodate an RNAV IAP with vertical guidance, usually provided by approach certified Baro-VNAV (Not found in light GA aircraft).
- o Requires a WAAS GPS.
- o LNAV/VNAV has a glide path.
- o The glide path guarantees vertical guidance over obstacles, but the DA may actually be higher than the LNAV MDA.
- o Use **"LNAV/VNAV DA"** approach minimums.

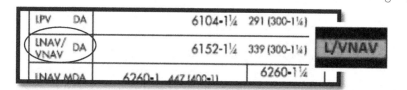

LPV DA		6104-1¼ 291 (300-1¼)	
LNAV/ DA VNAV		6152-1¼ 339 (300-1¼)	L/VNAV
LNAV MDA	6260-1 447 (400-1)	6260-1¼	

Although LNAV/VNAV and LPV approach minimums approximate ILS approach minimums, and Garmin refers to them as "precision approaches" with a Decision Altitude, the FAA considers them to be non-precision approaches. Technically, they are classified as an Approach with Vertical Guidance (APV).

100

LNAV+V – *Lateral Nav*igation + *Vertical Navigation*

o Requires a WAAS GPS.
o LNAV+V annunciation infers that RAIM is OK.
o Non-precision approach with an **advisory** glide slope.
o Unlike the LNAV/VNAV glide path, the LNAV+V advisory glide path doesn't guarantee obstacle clearance. Instead, it provides guidance for a stabilized approach, and meets the MDA at the approach's VDP.
o Use **"LNAV MDA"** approach minimums.

LNAV/VNAV DA	6152-1¼ 339 (300-1¼)		
LNAV MDA	6260-1 447 (400-1)	6260-1¼ 447 (400-1¼)	LNAV+V
CIRCLING	6440-1 555 (600-1)	6440-1½	

LNAV – *Lateral NAV*igation

LNAV/VNAV DA	6152-1¼ 339 (300-1¼)		
LNAV MDA	6260-1 447 (400-1)	6260-1¼ 447 (400-1¼)	LNAV
CIRCLING	6440-1 555 (600-1)	6440-1½	

o WAAS or non-WAAS GPS.
o Use **"LNAV MDA"** approach minimums.
o Garmin 430W/530W difference: The LNAV annunciation appears when flying an LNAV GPS approach, ILS, or VOR.

NOTE: If planning to fly an approach to LPV minimums, you should always be prepared for all the higher MDAs and DAs associated with the approach.

NOTE: LPV, L/VNAV, LNAV+V, or LNAV may not annunciate until the aircraft is two miles outside the FAF.

Baro – VNAV (Non-WAAS)

W11A	115°	Apt Elev	633	BUTLER COUNTY RGNL

▼ ⚠ If local altimeter setting not received, use Cincinnati Muni Airport-Lunken Field altimeter setting and increase all DAs 59 feet and all MDAs 60 feet. Baro-VNAV NA when using Cincinnati Muni Airport-Lunken Field altimeter setting. For uncompensated Baro-VNAV systems, LNAV/VNAV NA below -16°C (4°F) or above 47°C (116°F). Visibility reduction by helicopters NA. DME/DME RNP-0.3 NA.

References to "Baro-VNAV" are commonly found in approach notes. Baro-VNAV applies to aircraft with an FMS, where "Baro-VNAV" technology allows a non-WAAS GPS equipped aircraft to fly a VNAV approach.

DME Arc Approaches

- o Selecting an **IAF** from the approach menu, displays the arc on the GPS.
- o If you plan to be vectored to the final approach course, (no arcing), select "Vectors" from the approach menu.

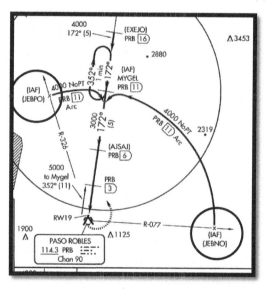

Reference this VOR/DME or GPS RWY 19 at KPRB, (Paso Robles, CA), there are two IAPs for the approach: **JEBNO** and **JEBPO**.

102

Finding Arc fixes for the GPS Arcing Approaches

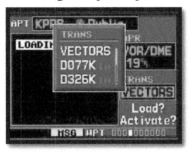

"JEBNO" and "JEBPO" cannot be found in the database. Instead, the choices are "D077K" and "D326K".

The VOR/DME or GPS RWY 19 approach uses the PRB 11 DME arc. Approach databases use a letter to represent the arc's DME. See the table below.

Letters for DME Arc Distances		
A = 1	B = 2	C = 3
D = 4	E = 5	F = 6
G = 7	H = 8	I = 9
J = 10	K = 11	L = 12
M = 13	N = 14	O = 15
. . . . etc.		

K is the 11th letter in the alphabet:
- o D077**K** means the 077° radial, **11 DME** (JEBNO).
- o D326**K** means the 326° radial, **11 DME** (JEBPO).

LDA with a Glide Slope

LDAs are in the database, but LDAs with a glide slope are <u>NOT</u>. You can still do something about that by using the LDA's identifier.
- o In the flight plan, insert the LDA identifier just before the airport identifier. For instance, I-ASO would be entered as "**IASO**", (drop the dash).
- o Set the inbound LDA's course in the "CRS" box.
- o Set the inbound LDA course in the OBS and press **OBS**. (This creates a magenta line for the GPS map.)

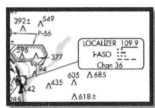

Terminal Arrival Areas (TAAs)

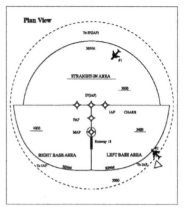

TAAs are not found on all RNAV procedures. However, when published, the TAA replaces the MSA for that approach procedure. The "T" design uses one to three IAFs. Some locations omit a right-base or left-base area due to airspace or terrain considerations. There's also an intermediate fix (IF) that also serves as an IAF. It has a final approach fix (FAF) and a missed approach point (MAP), which is usually located at the runway threshold.

Pilots entering the TAA, and cleared by air traffic control, are expected to proceed directly to the appropriate IAF associated with that area of the TAA, and at the altitude depicted, when within 30 NM of that fix. *(Ref. Dept. of Transportation, FAA, ATC Sect 8, 4-8-1)*

Finding Your Area

Reference the RNAV (GPS) RWY 21L, Prescott, Arizona (KPRC) – next page.
The DUKIW and AKUHY TAAs form two 90° pieces of the pie.

- o If flying a bearing of 90°, direct to DUKIW, you'd be in the **Right Base Area**.
- o Once in the DUKIW TAA, you are expected to descend to 9,600 feet.
- o If in the AKUHY TAA, (**Left Base Area**), you are expected to descend to 10,000 feet.
- o The PEVYU TAA (**Straight-in Area**), has two MSAs; 11,400 feet (30 to 12 miles from PEVYU), and 9,100, (12 miles from PEVYU).
- o Once passing DUKIW or AKUHY, note the 9,100' **NoPT** legs from DUKIW and AKUHY inbound to PEVYU.

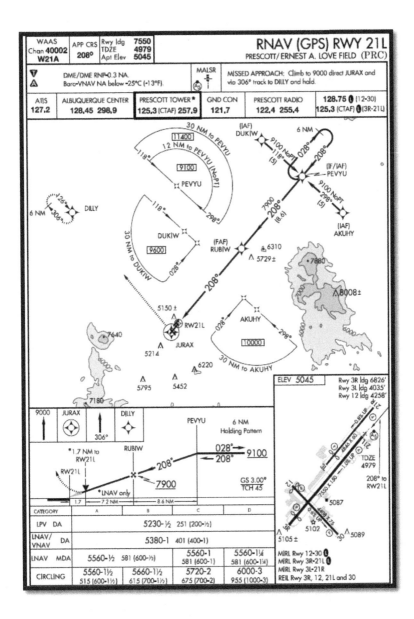

Hold in Lieu of Procedure Turns

Still referencing RNAV (GPS) RWY 21L – If you start the approach at the Intermediate Fix (IF) "*PEVYU*", note that there's a 4 nm race track pattern at *PEVYU*. **You MUST fly that pattern once**. (TAA pattern legs are defined in miles, not minutes).

If ATC does not want you to execute a procedure turn, the controller's clearance will be, "*Cleared direct PEVYU, maintain at or above nine thousand one hundred until PEVYU, cleared* **straight-in** *RNAV Runway Two One Left approach.*" *(Ref. Dept. of Transportation, FAA, ATC Sect 8, 4-8-1)*

"NoPT" at the IF/IAF

Some straight-in areas specify "NoPT".
Reference the RNAV GPS (RNAV) RWY 34 to Vernal, Utah (KVEL), shown below.

If you're higher than 10,000 feet crossing the IF/IAF "OHAPE", you could descend in the depicted racetrack, **but only if you've received permission from ATC.**

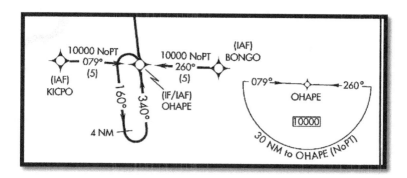

GNS 430 / 530 Missed Approach

o Brief the approach, scrolling through the approach and missed approach, checking for **conditional altitude requirements.** (Requirement to climb to an altitude before turning)

o Always press the *OBS* key to initiate the missed approach.

o After passing the missed approach point, *"SUSP"* always appears above the *OBS* key.

o After pressing *OBS*, *"SUSP"* will usually disappear and the course line for the missed approach will change from a thin line to a bold line.

• If you press *OBS*, and *"SUSP"* reappears, you have not made a mistake. Don't press the *OBS* key again, until you satisfy a **conditional altitude requirement.**

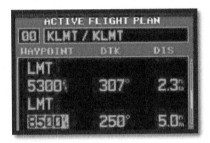

5,300 ft and 8,500 ft are missed approach **conditional altitude requirements** in this missed approach.

ILS Missed Approach Travel Tip

When performing a missed approach after a VOR, LOC or ILS approach, be sure to switch from the VOR or ILS/LOC signal, back to the GPS for missed approach guidance. (Press the CDI key).

Holding and Missed Approach Travel Tip
When holding is part of a missed approach procedure, the 430/530 and 430W/530W GPS units will remain "SUSPENDED" indefinitely.

AOPA's Air Safety Institute offers a course entitled **"IFR Chart Challenge: RNAV Approach"** and **"GPS for IFR Operations"**
These courses qualify for Wings Credit and AOPA Accident Forgiveness.

Being an airline pilot would be great if you didn't have to go on all those trips.

When Things Go Wrong

Priorities

Flying the airplane is more important than radioing your plight to a person on the ground – incapable of understanding or doing anything about it.

- ○ **Aviate**
- ○ **Navigate**, *then*
- ○ **Communicate**

Lost Communications or Degraded Capability, IFR

Lost Communications, VMC

Squawking 7600 is not always necessary, depending on your location. For example, in VMC weather, it's acceptable to land without squawking 7600. However, if you're near **controlled airspace**, squawking 7600 would be prudent.
In either case, land as soon as practical

Can you see why it's a good idea, during your preflight weather briefing, to learn about the closest VFR weather along your route of flight?

Lost Communications, IFR *(FAR 91.155)*

Squawk **7600**

ATC will try to contact you via:

- o The VOR's voice feature,
- o Other aircraft, *or*
- o By cell phone.

Lost Comm Memory Helpers

Continue on the ROUTE *via* AVE F :

- o **A**ssigned (Your last assigned heading)
- o **V**ectored (If nothing is assigned fly your last vector)
- o **E**xpected (If no vector, fly what was expected in your clearance)
- o **F**iled (Finally, fly what you filed)

Adjust the altitude *via* MEA – *this is* the *highest of:*

- o **M**EA
- o **E**xpected
- o **A**ssigned

Then, from the clearance limit fix, fly to the IAF and begin the approach as close as possible to the Expect Further Clearance time (**EFC**). If you don't have an EFC, use the **ETA**.

Lost Radio Contact on the Airways

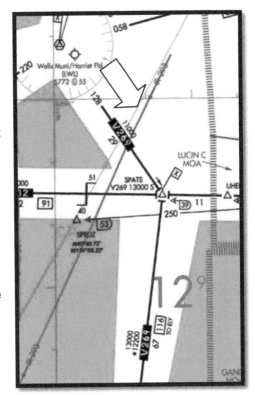

Situation:

Proceeding Southwest on V269 at 11,000 feet MSL. Up ahead at **SPATS**, there's a 13,000' mandatory crossing altitude.

Calls to Salt Lake Center, requesting a higher altitude, are unanswered. Zero contact with Salt Lake ARTCC and the MCA at SPATS looms ahead.

What should you do?

Answer: Squawk 7600, and start a climb so as to cross SPATS at or above 13,000 feet MSL. If V269 had a higher MEA South of SPATS, then, at or before reaching SPATS, you would continue climbing to the new MEA.

What should you do if you can't reach 13,000 feet by SPATS?

Answer: Hold over SPATS in a standard pattern on course (on V269), until reaching 13,000 MSL, then continue South on V269.

Lost Comm – After Takeoff

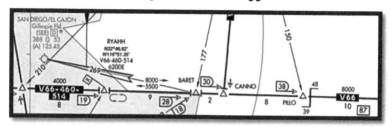

Situation: Takeoff weather – 400 overcast, 1 mile visibility and light rain. Before departing San Diego's Gillespie field (SEE), you call for an IFR clearance, and receive: "Cleared to the Phoenix Sky Harbor airport via V-66, then as filed. Climb and maintain 3,000, expect 9,000 10 minutes after departure."
Gillespie Tower instructs, "Turn left heading 130, cleared for takeoff runway 27R."

You're in the clouds at 500 feet and after 4 minutes of flying, you experience communications failure. Your altitude is 3,000 feet and heading is still 130°.

The MEA along our route starts at 4,000, and you must cross Ryahh at 6,200. After RYAHH, the MEA increases to 8,000. What should you do?

Squawk 7600, and then apply "AVE F"to the route:

A – You were assigned heading 130, so continue to fly that heading for now.
V – In your limited communication with the controller, you never received radar vectors.
E – Your clearance instructed you to fly V-66 then as filed.
F – After you fly what was expected, (V-66), then you'll fly what you filed.

Continue to fly heading 130 until you intercept V-66 and proceed on your flight planned route.

Apply "MEA", to the altitude, flying the highest of::

- o **M** – Minimum en-route altitude (4,000, but you must cross RYAHH at 6,200 feet).
- o **E** – Expected (9,000).
- o **A** – Assigned – You were not assigned another altitude by another controller.

After 10 minutes of flying, depart 3,000 and begin a climb to 9,000 feet.

If not at or above 6,200 by RYAHH, hold at RYAHH until at or above 6,200, and then proceed East on V66, continuing the climb to 9,000 (the MEA is 8,000 East bound on V66).

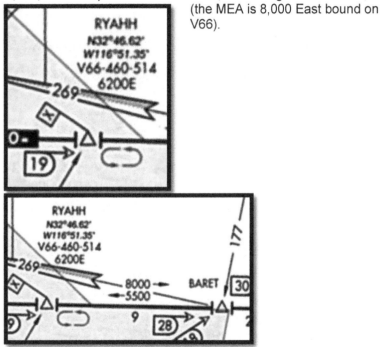

Lost Communications, Landing VMC at a Controlled Airport

- o Remain outside or above Class D airspace until you determine the direction of traffic and runway in use.
- o Squawk 7600 before entering Class D airspace.
- o Enter the traffic pattern downwind on "a 45", and fly a typical pattern for landing.
- o Look for the Tower's light gun signals.

Lost Communications, Landing VMC at an Uncontrolled Airport

- o Overfly the airport 500 feet above pattern altitude.
- o Look for traffic, wind direction, and runway in use.
- o Enter the traffic pattern downwind on "a 45", and fly a typical pattern for landing.

Loss of Navigation Capability *(FAR 91.187)*

Report the loss to ATC along with the degree to which it has affected your ability to operate IFR in the ATC system.

Loss of PFD/MFD or Autopilot
(Primary Flight Display / Multi-Function Display)

If you have a PFD or MFD, you should know what a failure looks like and the application of procedures to continue safely.

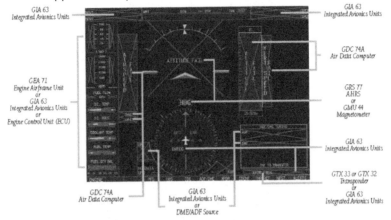

The Air Data Computer (ADC) provides altitude and airspeed information to PFDs and the **autopilot**.

Loss of a Vacuum Pump

Loss of Attitude Indicator and Heading Indicator

Is this a reason to declare an emergency if you're IMC? Absolutely! You've lost *Navigation Capability*.

Experience is a hard teacher. First comes the test, then the lesson.

115

Pitot Static Problems

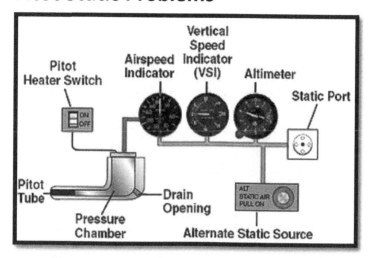

Malfunction: Pitot tube is blocked.

The airspeed drops to zero. Pressure in the Pitot system escapes through the drain hole.

ACTION: Pitot Heat — ON.

Malfunction: Pitot tube and the drain hole are blocked.

Pressure remains trapped in the system, and the airspeed indication increases and decreases with altitude, acting like an altimeter.

ACTION: Pitot Heat — ON. (Try to melt the object blocking the holes).

Malfunction: Static port is blocked.

The altimeter freezes and the VVI/VSI indicates "zero" or is faulty. As altitude increases, the airspeed indicates LOWER than normal. As altitude decreases, the airspeed indicates HIGER than normal.

ACTION: Use the Alternate Static Air Control, or break the glass on altimeter or VVI/VSI. Alternate air, when vented to the slightly lower pressure in the cabin, causes possible increases in:

- Airspeed (+ 5 to 10 knots), *and*
- Altitude (+ 25 to 75 feet).

Electrical Failure

Affects the turn coordinator, HSI, some attitude indicators, and the instrument lights.

Unusual Attitudes and Recoveries

(Attitude and Heading indicators inoperative)

If the nose is low:

- Reduce power to prevent excessive airspeed and altitude loss.

- Using the Turn and center the aileron and Coordinator, level the wings ball by applying coordinated rudder pressures.
- Apply elevator pressure, correcting the pitch attitude to level flight.

If the nose is high:

- Apply power and forward elevator pressure to lower the nose and prevent a stall
- Apply coordinated aileron and rudder pressure to correct the bank.

- Using the Turn Coordinator, level the wings and center the ball by applying coordinated aileron and rudder pressures.
- When at a safe airspeed, with full control of the aircraft, start a climb or descent to the original altitude and heading.

 *Do not trust or use the attitude indicator until you verify that it's reliable. Cover the bad instruments so you won't be tempted to use them.*

Partial panel – Vacuum Pump Failure

  Classic Heading and Attitude indicators are usually powered by the vacuum pump.

 The turn coordinator is usually electrically powered, allowing you to find wings level should the vacuum pump fail.

When a vacuum pump fails, the attitude indicator displays the wrong pitch, and eventually manifests a nose low bank.

 Use the airspeed indicator, IVI/VVI, altimeter, and turn coordinator to verify a pump failure and discover the faulty or inoperative instrument.

Ask ATC for Help

- o Get vectors to VFR conditions
- o If you can't be led to VFR conditions, ask ATC to avoid altitude and course changes.
- o Partial panel approaches are difficult, but possible.
- o No gyro approaches (ASR/PAR) are a good IFR option.

 *There are some flight instructors who feel that the student is important, and there are some instructors who feel that the instructor is important. Pick carefully.*

Minimum/Emergency Fuel (AIM)

Declaring minimum fuel indicates that when reaching the destination, you can accept little or no delay. ATC does not give your aircraft priority because you haven't declared an emergency. Min Fuel is merely an advisory that <u>if</u> you are delayed, you'll probably declare an emergency.

Upon initial contact with ATC, add "Minimum Fuel" to your call sign. If you burn into your RESERVE FUEL, that's not a reason to declare Minimum Fuel, unless you don't expect a safe landing to occur soon.

Emergency fuel indicates that you have declared an emergency and you require and expect priority handling. Upon initial contact with ATC, add "Emergency Fuel" to your call sign, along with the fuel remaining in minutes.

Do you know what fuel state would encourage you to declare:

- o   Minimum Fuel?
- o   Emergency Fuel?

The emergencies you train for almost never happen. It's the one you can't train for that kills you.
— *Ernest K. Gann, advice from the 'Old Pelican,' 'The Black Watch,' 1989.*

120

Other books by James D Price

Flight Review Study Guide will be the first thing you open when getting ready for any pilot proficiency training. Wings flights, or BFR. – everything is covered. The **Flight Review Study Guide** is also an indispensable cross county flight-planning handbook. You'll fly with confidence and you'll be a better pilot.

ISBN 978-1-938586-81-1

Aircraft Expense Tracking - Single or Multi, Sole Owner or Club. Aircraft Expense Tracking will help you keep perfect records. You can record aircraft squawks, and keep track of maintenance and oil changes. There's even a spot to record VOR checks and GPS data updates each month.

With **Aircraft Expense Tracking,** you'll always know when inspections are due, how much your aircraft costs per year, and you'll be ready for taxes with business and charitable deductions.

ISBN 978-1-938586-80-4

For more information, visit Jim's website at:

http://www.JDPriceCFI.com

Printed in the U.S.A.
http://www.WritersCramp.us

CPSIA information can be obtained
at www.ICGtesting.com
Printed in the USA
BVOW05s0941280217
R7843900001B/R78439PG476875BVX1B/1/P